• DREW MACARTHUR ELICKER • Seattle • Washington • Summer • 1979 •

COLOR, FORM AND SPACE

COLOR, FORM AND SPACE

FABER BIRREN

 REINHOLD PUBLISHING CORPORATION • NEW YORK

ACKNOWLEDGMENTS

Thanks are expressed to Armand Fiorenza for the design of the plastic forms. Most of the black and white drawings are by LaVerne Bovee. The color photographs are by J. Walter Grimm.

DESIGNED BY MYRON HALL III
TYPESETTING AND PRINTING BY THE COMET PRESS, INC.
COLOR PRINTING BY HOLYOKE LITHOGRAPH CO.
BOUND BY RUSSELL-RUTTER COMPANY, INC.

Contents

List of Plates

Foreword

Color is not separate; it is integral. It is not surface; it is substance. It is primary in human sensation, for everything seen by the eye—space included—is colored. Experience of it is constant, even with the eyes closed and in total darkness.

This book is a companion volume to the author's *Creative Color*, in which new visual and psychological principles were described and illustrated. Here, however, probably for the first time, departure is into the realm of three dimensions. What is to be said of color in the plastic arts? What is its significance in terms of form and space?

The artist today owes a great debt to the Gestalt psychologist whose inquiries into the mysteries of perception have laid bare a long series of facts which have gone unrecognized through the centuries. Because of him, the artist can actually "see" better and gain a vision which was denied even the greatest creators of the past. Although knowledge of the dynamic properties of vision cannot substitute for individual talent, surely the artist can profit from it and propel himself into a new and exciting future.

Much art of the past is admired today for its craftsmanship. In painting one marvels at the perfection of technique and mastery of details. Much of architecture—Greek, Gothic, Oriental—is extraordinary in its intricacy and elegance. No man of modern times could vie with much of this. He would be unoriginal to copy it, and it is doubtful if he would have the time.

It is probably even futile to grieve about it, as some do. After all, if the teachings of the Gestalt psychologist are fairly comprehended, it is easy to appreciate that the ancient was an ordinary man like his living counterpart. If he was extraordinary at all, it was due not so much to his insight as to his application.

What is different—and largely tragic—is that art today seeks individuality in a society that has little sympathy for it. Everyone is to be unique, and yet the major forces of life move in a contrary way like a tide and constantly beach the artist and knock the wind out of him.

"Art in the fullest sense of the term is the knowledge and understanding of man," wrote Keyserling. And man's identification begins with himself. The wonderful thing about perception is that every man is endowed with it. If the artist is to reach new frontiers, he may go back into the past for a bit of history, but he will be lost among ruins if he stays there.

This book attempts to push into the future. It deals with color, form and space. It points out that if there is anything to beauty, it is in the eye of the beholder. Beauty is not the intrinsic property of natural or man-made things, but of the human eye and brain. This is an important fact to grasp, and I have tried my best to clarify it.

The relationships of color and form are demonstrated in numerous black and white and color illustrations. Because I am dealing with plastic forms reproduced on flat pages, I have built models and photographed them in an effort to suggest three dimensions. The results have been fairly successful.

Most of all, I have endeavored to present new concepts and to encourage what I believe to be a more personal and revealing approach to art forms, drawn from the most fecund of all sources—man's own perception.

FABER BIRREN

1.

The Perception

of Forms in Space

Many architects and designers have two curious faculties not shared by average persons. The first is the ability—through training and concentration—to visualize shapes and forms as if they existed in empty space. Architects and designers, bent over drawing boards, deal with free invention, putting lines to paper as a dreamer might trace castles in his imagination.

In actuality, however, all space is filled—even if only with air. And in perception, a sense of space gives reality to what the eyes sees. Man lives in space (as well as time) and is never without an awareness of it. As James J. Gibson writes, "The suggestion is that *visual* space, unlike abstract geometrical space, is perceived only by virtue of what fills it." A building, or a washing machine, is never isolated from its environment or the space it fills. The thinking process, if it attempts to separate space from form, deludes itself in an impossible feat. Many a conception that has looked good on "paper" has suffered when exposed to the world itself. As a matter of fact, many a form, originally shaped without immediate reference to environment, has required correction and alteration to make it fit where it was meant to belong.

Secondly, it is by no means rare for architects to deal with forms as if they were colorless. In other words, all consideration may be given to line, mass, proportion as things in themselves. Yet it is completely true that nothing seen by the eye is colorless. Color is integral with form and cannot be divorced from it. White, gray, black are *colors* for the simple reason that they are definite and positive in perception. And they convey visual and emotional messages which are far from neutral. White may be "light" and stark, gray sober, black "heavy" and forlorn. Surely the spiritual beauty of

Gothic architecture is complemented by the sympathetic mood of gray stone and marble. It would be most difficult to express moods of levity or sensuous pleasure with gray—regardless of how amusing or whimsical the artist attempted to be with design factors alone.

According to Gibson, the visual world "is extended in distance and modeled in depth; it is upright, stable, and without boundaries; it is colored, shadowed, illuminated and textured; it is composed of surfaces, edges, shapes, and interspaces; and most important of all, it is filled with things which have meaning."

It has taken the Gestalt psychologist to deal with and explain this *meaning*. According to M. Wertheimer, who is credited with the development of Gestalt theory, "A Gestalt is a whole whose characteristics are determined, not by the characteristics of its individual elements, but by the internal nature of the whole."

The reader who is unfamiliar with Gestalt psychology will profit from this fresh and human viewpoint—one that has accomplished wonders in explaining the nature of form and color perception and in extending the boundaries of art to farther horizons.

"The whole is more than the sum of its separate parts."—Katz.

"To apply the Gestalt category means to find out which parts of nature belong as parts to functional wholes."—Koffka.

As an introduction to the modern Gestalt approach, we shall examine briefly some of the ideas of ancient times. They will provide a background for insight into the principles of Gestalt psychology.

It is quite obvious that the builders of ancient Egypt and Asia Minor had

Figure 1. The solids of Pythagoras.

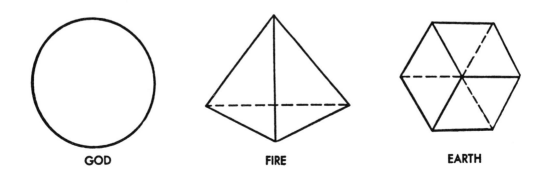

GOD   FIRE   EARTH

a magnificent understanding of architectural proportion and form, although their theories in the matter are little known. It was the Greeks—notably Pythagoras—who related beauty to mathematics and looked upon harmony as a key to the universe. Pythagoras discovered the diatonic scale in music and noted that only five solids existed whose sides and angles were all equal. (See Figure 1.) These he related to the Greek elements. They were the simplest and most perfect of forms. Earth particles were symbolized by the cube, this solid having the greatest stability. Fire particles were associated with the tetrahedron, a form comprised of four equilateral triangles; air particles with the octahedron, a double pyramid; and water particles with the icosahedron, a solid having twenty equilateral triangles for its faces.

A fifth solid, the dodecahedron, the most complex of all, was related to the fifth element of the Greek Mysteries, the ether. The sphere, perfect among all symmetrical solids, was reserved for the deity. The solids of Pythagoras were also symbolized by colors.

It should be understood that beauty, form, mathematics, music were all involved with Greek philosophy and mysticism. They all held keys to the secrets of the universe and led undoubtedly to the perfection of Greek architectural proportion.

During the Renaissance, there was a revival of interest in Greek philosophy and mathematics. The Italian Alberti, for example, developed a theory that the Pythagorean intervals in music could be adapted to architectural design. Bertrand Russell writes, "A grasp of the numerical structure in things thus conferred on man new powers over his surroundings. In a way it made man more like God."

AIR WATER ETHER

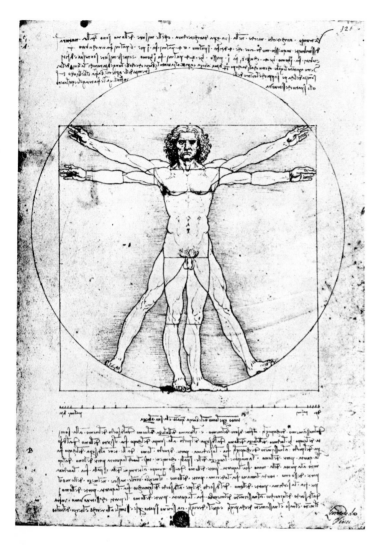

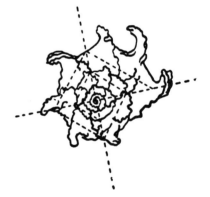

Figure 2. The geometric proportions of man according to Leonardo da Vinci.

Figure 3. Dynamic symmetry in nature. After Jay Hambidge.

Figure 4. Geometric design. After Claude Bragdon.

Figure 5. The geometry of beauty. After Claude Bragdon.

Indeed man himself could be used as a measure. Within him was a small universe—the microcosm—and even his height, breadth and proportion were fittingly adapted to harmony in art. Figure 2, taken from a pen and ink drawing of Leonardo da Vinci, diagrams man's geometric proportions in terms of a square and a circle.

Mathematics and geometry in Greek art and architecture have been given elaborate study. Two good sources here are the works of Jay Hambidge on *Dynamic Symmetry* and Claude Bragdon on *Projective Ornament*. Hambidge writes, "The basic principles underlying the greatest art so far produced in the world may be found in the proportions of the human figure and in the growing plant." This is the Greek tradition. (See Figure 3.) To this Bragdon adds, "Geometry is an inexhaustible well of formal beauty from which to fill our bucket; but before the draught is fit for use, it should be examined, analyzed, and filtered through the consciousness of the artist." (See Figures 4, 5, 6.)

Figure 6. Rhythm and harmony in the geometric cube. After Claude Bragdon.

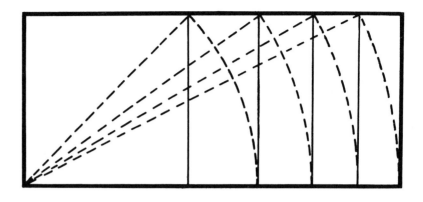

Figure 7. The Root Rectangles of Jay Hambidge.

Figure 7 shows the "Root Rectangles" presented by Hambidge as the basis of classical Greek proportion. (Figure 8 illustrates an adaptation to a Greek drinking cup.) In the light of modern research in Gestalt psychology, the observations of Hambidge and Bragdon are hardly to be doubted. But is it Greek proportion that is beautiful—or is it the eye (and brain) which finds beauty in such arrangements? The answer is probably both.

In modern times some of the Post-Impressionist painters—notably the Cubists—sought to reduce nature to geometry and to create illusions of depth on flat canvases. Cézanne declared, "Nature must be treated through the cylinder, the sphere, the cone." Like the Greeks he felt that nature hid secrets which he set forth to discover—overlooking the more personal truth that laws of beauty necessarily lie within man's own consciousness. Braque allied painting to architecture, using lines, planes and geometric shapes to create

Figure 8. Dynamic symmetry in a Greek vase. After Jay Hambidge.

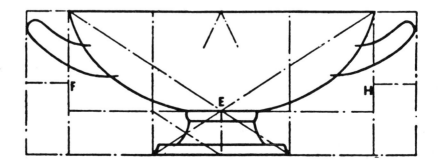

illusions of plastic space. Picasso, in his Cubist period, tried to imply volume on a flat plane without resorting to light and shade or even perspective.

However, it would be a mistake for the artist to fail to recognize human factors in the perception of space and form. It would be equally incongruous to assume that beauty is the secret property of nature, or that it comes through some vague and mysterious inspiration, or that it is somehow unrelated to human reactions. Arnheim in his remarkable book, *Art and Visual Perception*, writes, "The exalted kind of seeing that leads to the creation of great art appears as an outgrowth of the humbler and more common activity of the eyes in everyday life."

How is perception organized? Why does man see the way he does, and why, in turn, is beauty more likely to be found in the eye of the beholder than in the thing beyond? According to Gestalt theory, "There is no form apart from the subject who forms it." (W. Stern.) Man's sense of beauty is not wholly a matter of inspiration or cultural training, natural law or mathematics. If he happens to see beauty in certain symmetrical arrangements, this is not because there are any hard and fast principles in nature aside from human consciousness, but that perception itself, the eye-brain of man, holds responsibility for everything. If there are any eternal elements of harmony, they owe their origin to human consciousness—and Gestalt psychology knows a lot about them. Study here may well lead to a free expression that departs radically from the fixed and static conventions of antiquity.

Gestalt psychology was made famous a decade or two ago by Max Wertheimer, Wolfgang Köhler, Kurt Koffka, David Katz and others. Although their investigations dealt mainly with visual perception, the Gestalt viewpoint has now been blended into virtually all branches of psychology. To the artist or architect, it represents the most important and fruitful field of inquiry in many a generation. For it has reappraised and discovered much about man and the processes and motivations that give order to his world. As Köhler puts it, "Organization in the sensory field originates as a characteristic achievement of the nervous system." Beauty (or ugliness) is not out *there* in man's environment, but *here* within man's brain. Where formerly man strove to find laws of symmetry, balance, harmony and the like in nature, he now may be sure (thanks to the Gestalt psychologist) that such are his endowments, not nature's. Bear in mind that nature is full of endless shapes and forms. Man is the one who is exacting about them, for all in nature is by no means considered beautiful. Let me present a couple of examples of man's sense of art.

*Figure 9. Japanese print
in which perception is invited to go far beyond
what has actually been
put down by the artist.*

In a Japanese print or painting, what is actually in evidence is a sheet of paper containing certain lines, graduations and colors, nothing more. (See Figure 9.) Yet perception adds beauty, a sense of atmosphere, space, density, perspective. And the artist is great who can convey these illusions most effectively.

On the other hand, let us consider the symmetrical ornaments of Greek architecture. (See Figure 10.) Beauty was thought to be in the form, design or pattern. It became the property of the materials into which the Greek designer put his handiwork. He apparently searched for natural laws, perhaps overlooking the fact that it was he who put the laws into nature, and not nature that revealed the laws to him. Certainly he, as well as modern artists, handled ornament as substance in itself, often putting it in remote places where the eyes of man haven't had much chance to see it. Is a Greek fret at roof level on a multi-story skyscraper beautiful if the passing viewer cannot see it?

Beauty, harmony, rhythm, proportion, color, form and space are not the properties of things but of human perception. What you see literally or

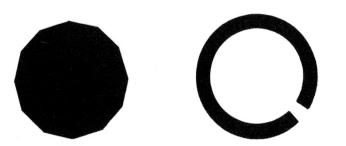

what actually exists in the external world is not the true substance of perception but only the stimulus for it. To answer an old enigma, there is no sound when a tree falls in a forest and no one is near. There may be vibrations in the air, but the word *sound* specifically relates to sensation. The same is true of color. A surface may reflect light energy in certain ways, but color itself is human experience. As will be seen in later chapters, a surface reflecting an unvarying light may have widely different appearances. Properties of color or beauty are not in external things but in the dynamics of seeing. Appreciate the magic role of human perception, and creative art may break through to new frontiers.

Wilhelm Ostwald, the color theorist, was concerned with the psychological and perceptual elements of design and form. In his book on the harmony of form (1922), he noted the following: If a dot is presented in a small and irregular way, it seems to lack simple conviction and requires some explanation for the viewer to be satisfied. If, however, the dot is presented in the form of a circle, square or hexagon, questions are not necessary—these forms appear right and normal. (See Figure 11.) Further, if a simple form such as a T square is slightly tilted, such obliqueness may seem more arbitrary than natural. Yet when the T square is oriented to a straight position, either on its edge or corner, the result is quite satisfactory. Thus A in Figure 12 is stable and well-oriented, while B is off balance and dynamic.

The most satisfactory forms are the simple ones—the square or cube, circle or sphere, triangle or pyramid, etc. The visual process is one that seems to demand and prefer simplicity. Forms that are slightly irregular or which have gaps in them will appear quite regular or complete on short exposure or in their afterimages. (See Figure 13.)

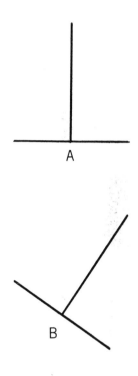

Figure 12. A is stable, while B is dynamic.

Figure 13. Slightly irregular forms will be seen as regular in afterimages.

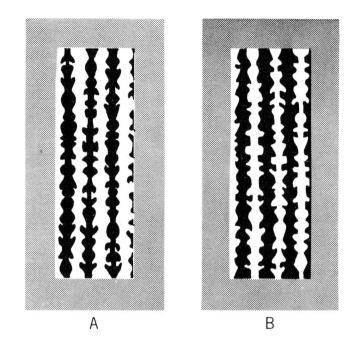

Figure 14. The insistence of symmetrical forms over asymmetrical. Concentration will be on black in A and on white in B. After Koffka.

A   B

Wertheimer noted that an angle somewhat more or less than 90 degrees would be seen as a perfect right angle when briefly exposed. Triangles and squares (or pyramids and cubes), incidentally, are easier to perceive and orient in space than is a circle or sphere. This may be because the sphere lacks sharpness and is not easy for the eye to focus on. The moon on the horizon may appear to be merely a few miles away (and relatively large). High in the sky, its distance may seem farther (and its size smaller).

So it is that perception itself works toward simplicity. It strives to make irregular shapes appear regular, to look for symmetry and balance. Figure 14 illustrates an experiment described by Koffka, showing the insistence of simple and symmetrical forms over asymmetrical forms. The eye forever seeks symmetrical forms and concentrates on them.

Probably the experience that is basic to man's preference for simple form relates to his natural sense of equilibrium. Kepes writes, "We cannot bear chaos—the disturbance of equilibrium in the field of experience." The eye struggles hard to bring the object of its interest into the center of its field of view and then to see it clearly, distinctly and in right balance.

Everyone will recognize this as part of his own nature. The psychologist defines motivation as "the disequilibrium of the organism which leads to action for the restoration of stability." (L. L. Whyte.) A picture askew on the wall may distress some individuals. Yet the same persons may look at the same picture with their heads tilted and think nothing of it. Swinging in a garden may be a pleasurable experience, for the world remains stable as you float to and fro. But if you remained still and the world began to swing, you would be quite uneasy, if not nauseated.

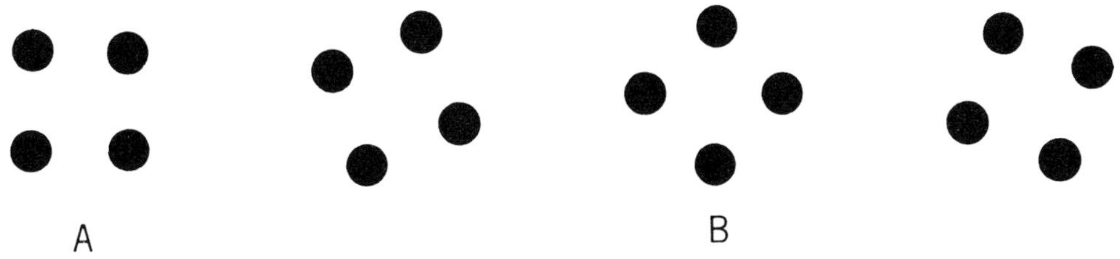

Figure 15. Experiment devised by Katz. Arrangements A and B will be preferred.

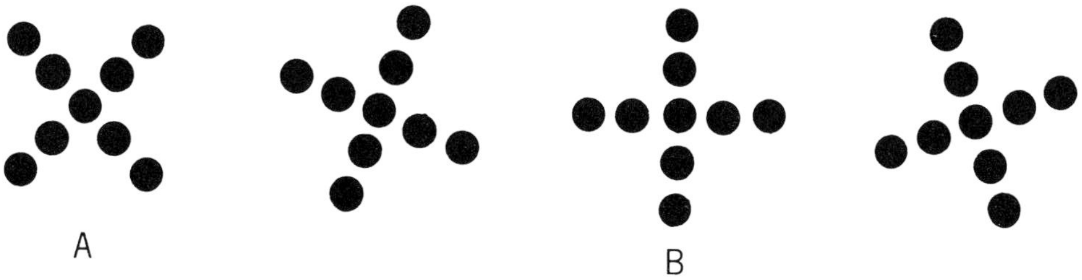

Figure 16. In these arrangements, positions A and B will be preferred. After Katz.

Refer to Figure 15 which illustrates an experiment devised by David Katz. Four cylindrical forms were placed on a revolving surface. A group of adults were then given similar forms and asked to place them on an adjacent table. The revolving cylinders were never at rest. Most of the subjects placed the cylinders as in position A; a few as in position B. According to Katz, "No other variations occurred."

Where nine cylinders were used (see Figure 16), the subjects arranged them in position A more often than in position B, and again no other variations were set up. It would appear that the eye likes the horizontal position best and the vertical position next.

Man wants the world to be stable. And he wants things to appear well-adjusted to the natural forces of gravity. The world doesn't shake when he shakes his head, nor does it twist about when he lies down. As Gibson describes, you cannot make an object jump by glancing rapidly from one side of it to the other. But quick pressure with your finger through the lid on the outer corner of your eye will cause obvious movement in objects before you. Similarly, the world remains upright even when you lie down and look at it. However, your judgment of the vertical will be more accurate when you are standing or sitting up rather than reclining.

What, then, are the chief attributes of form and space in human perception?

Simple forms are the easiest to perceive, the most stable and "pleasing." They resist alteration by the observer and maintain their character even when seen momentarily or in afterimages.

However, movement may be necessary for the form to become truly

Figure 17. Superimposed prints of Radio City. Perception is disturbed where forms are not aligned with natural forces.

revealed. Even the formless pattern of trees in winter may fall into planes and three dimensions as the eye shifts. Experiments have shown that form recognition by animals (dogs) is far easier if they are permitted to move about and not held in one position. The experience of form is therefore dynamic and not static.

Good forms are stable forms. The Leaning Tower of Pisa may be an amusing novelty, but Radio City in the same predicament would be disturbing indeed. (See Figure 17.) To sensitive individuals, the slanting floors of a rickety or termite-ridden barn may cause seasickness and nausea. (Once again, generalities are being expressed. Much non-objective art deliberately violates or upsets these principles. However, this art is a personal expression which often deliberately contradicts the usual reactions of most people.)

In the perception of forms in space, the eye maintains what are termed shape consistency and size consistency. Solid forms keep their proper shape when see at different angles. (See Figure 18.) A perfect circle or square will not become an oval or a rectangle as it is swung about and foreshortened. Even an oval or a rectangle cannot be made to look like a circle or a square. (See Figure 19.) This is especially true of forms seen with other objects which also are familiar. However, if such experiments are performed in total darkness, and the forms shown on an illuminated screen, the "sense" of shape consistency may be confused and lost. Here circles or disks are more difficult to perceive in true form because of their lack of angular shape.

As to size consistency, Vernon writes, "It appears that in general, in normal everyday experience, the decrease in size of the retinal image of a receding object appears as an increase of distance and not as a decrease in its size. Clearly then, for the phenomenon to appear, the observer must have some knowledge of the size of the object when it is close to him, or at least some means of judging its distance."

In architecture, effects of distance may be emphasized. It is common practice, for example, to increase the height of lower floors of a building and to decrease the height of upper stories. This makes for a wholly natural effect which agrees with average experiences in perception.

Certain arrangements, proportions, intervals appear pleasing where they follow what seem to be geometric laws. This has been identified with Greek

Figure 18. Experiment in shape constancy, using regular disks and squares.

Figure 19. Experiment in shape constancy, using ovals and rectangles.

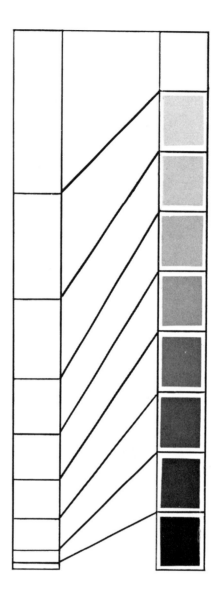

Figure 20. At right is a scale of logarithmic intervals which show the increase in increments of white which when added to black produce a gray scale of visually equal steps (shown at far right.)

architecture and with the Root Rectangles of Jay Hambidge (Figure 7). However, such beauty is not a divine or natural property of nature but a phenomenon of human perception.

Simplicity, order, symmetry, as found in nature, are functionally related to physical structure, growth patterns and the like. If they are beautiful, it is that human perception finds them so. (Remember that nature can be "ugly" too.) Beauty is not intrinsic in nature; if anywhere, it is intrinsic in human consciousness. This was the remarkable discovery of Ernst Weber (1795-1878) and Gustav Fechner (1801-1887). It was the struggle of both men to find a relationship between external physical facts and human consciousness. Their dream was to make psychology an exact science and to use scientific measurements to deal with what were thought to be purely spiritual or emotional qualities. While the ambition failed in many respects, it constitutes one of the great achievements in the field of psychology.

In essence, the Weber-Fechner Law states that the intensity of a sensation increases as the logarithm of the strength of the stimulus. The law strives to correlate physical stimuli with psychical or mental experience. It is approximately accurate as applied to the senses of sight, hearing, pressure and sound but is somewhat limited as applied to the chemical senses of taste and smell.

Figure 20 shows a lineal representation of logarithmic intervals (in lines) which correspond to the proportions of white (added to black) that are necessary to produce a gray scale having perceptually equal steps. The two bands —one concerned with gray values and the other with space intervals—are notably and sympathetically beautiful.

As may be noted in the scale at the left, small amounts of white are needed, when added to black, to produce noticeable gradations at the bottom of the gray scale. These additions of white have to be increased in logarithmic proportion as lighter values are reached. When the same exact figures are converted to space intervals, using lines, two scales—concerned with two different visual experiences—bear similar impressions of beauty.

Thus, in the Weber-Fechner Law, nature loses face as the precursor or sovereign of beauty. If there is beauty in nature, it exists pre-born within the consciousness of man.

Ostwald stated that the division of forms into intervals cannot be haphazard if the human eye is to be satisfied. In Figure 21, regular intervals (A) appear satisfactory, while haphazard intervals (B) may appear disturbing. Great beauty and grace follows the logarithmic interval (C). (The reader may prefer the haphazard interval if he wishes. The point here is not one of esthetics or taste but of fundamental reactions typical of average persons.)

Symmetrical forms hold greater interest and are more insistent in perception than irregular or asymmetric forms. This was shown in Figure 14. It is now pertinent to deal with the figure-ground phenomenon set forth by E. Rubin. In describing Rubin's work, Vernon writes, "The first essential stage in perception is the emergence of one principal part of the field which is the 'figure' from the remainder which is the 'ground.'" This is worthy of elaboration.

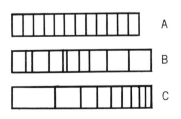

Figure 21. Regular or logarithmic intervals will be preferred to haphazard ones. After Ostwald.

Figure 22. The figure-ground phenomenon of Rubin. The central figure always persists and will look superimposed on the ground.

Refer to Figure 22. In each of the three sketches the geometrical floral pattern is seen as the figure, while the space around it appears as the ground —regardless of size. This seems to involve a basic law of perception. Now the figure is likely to look as if superimposed, to be solid and highly structured, while the ground may be more filmy and vague. The figure, in a word, stands out, and the ground retires. This is particularly true if the figure is convex in shape rather than concave, as will be brought out in the following paragraphs.

In architectural design, Rubin's law is quite pertinent. Detail, clarity of shape, nearness will be associated with the figure, while peripheral things (the ground) will be less significant. Refer to Figure 23. A will perhaps look more natural than B. In A, the figure has detail and seems properly formed and well-defined. In B, the detail is in the wrong place and the tree shape looks as if it were cut out and empty. There may be some relationship between the figure-ground phenomenon and the fact that foveal vision (central) is clearer and more distinct than peripheral vision.

Figure 23. A appears more natural than B.

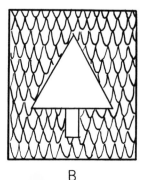

A B

Figure 24. A looks super-imposed; B looks like a hole.

A   B

In architecture, windows that look into interior space seem to run contrary to the figure-ground phenomenon. The portholes of a ship are obviously and functionally holes. Architects of the past have used ornate window frames, sills and lintels to make windows more prominent. Gothic architects blended walls with windows by introducing narrow bands and strips. Both devices help tie the frame into the window and bring the window forward, thus relating it to the figure of the building rather than letting it recede into the walls or fall back of them.

Related to the figure-ground phenomenon is the matter of convexity and concavity, also investigated by Rubin. According to Rubin, convexity tends to win out over concavity. In Figure 24, convexity makes for a better figure than concavity. A looks better than B. A looks superimposed, while B resembles a hole. At the same time, A is softer and has a better tactile quality, while B is sharp and pointed.

Now study Figure 25. In A, convexity tends to expand, to be soft and billowing. B tends to contract and to have apparently sharp edges. As applied

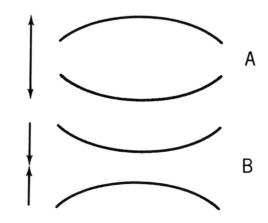

Figure 25. Convexity tends to expand, while concavity contracts.

A

B

*Figure 26. Traditional
shapes in architectural
forms.*

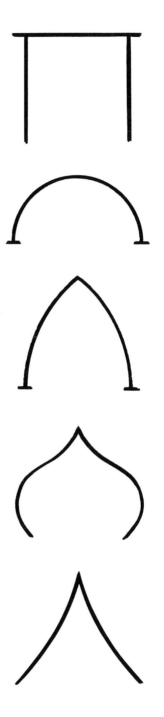

to architectural forms, A is generally more pleasant than B. Traditionally most buildings of monumental design have been based on convex shapes. Figure 26 shows outlines that are characteristic of ancient buildings, Roman, Gothic, Oriental. The bottom form is not often found and resembles a tent.

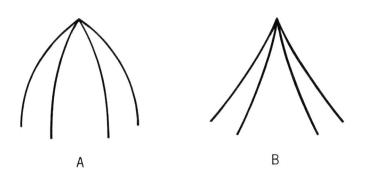

B

Figure 27. Most persons will prefer the expanding form A to the collapsing form B.

Yet there is a tendency in modern architecture to glorify the concave. Compare A and B in Figure 27. One swells out, the other curves in. According to Gestalt principles, A would be more pleasant than B—whether seen from the outside or inside.

A building designed as in B of Figure 27 would violate what most persons look upon as agreeable form. Claustrophobia is associated with confined spaces from which there is no escape. It is quite easy to provoke a feeling of horror by tales of buildings that collapse or mine shafts that cave in.

A church based on the convex form shown in A of Figure 27 would seem lofty. It would tend to expand and reach upward toward the sky. A church that followed the convex form shown in B would contract, crowd in on the viewer and sink down toward earth, rather than up toward heaven. One wonders if architects who apply the concave form have a good understanding of instinctive factors in human perception or whether they are merely trying to be different.

In common experience, most things—the human body, rocks, clouds, hills and the like—are largely convex in shape. Maybe because of this, convex shapes are better liked. In Figure 28, the geometric form looks rigid (A). The convex form (B) will probably be found to have more grace than the concave form (C).

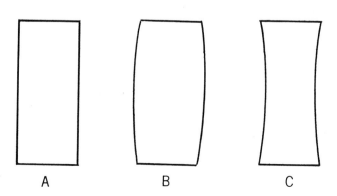

A

B

C

Figure 28. Modifications of a cylindrical or rectangular form.

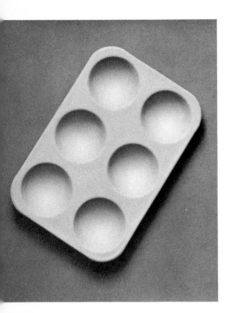

Figure 29. The six cups look indented, but if the page is turned upside down, they will bulge out.

The appearance of convexity or concavity seems to depend quite a bit on illumination. (See Figure 29.) Light normally comes from above. Convex forms will have shadows at the bottom, while concave forms will have shadows at the top. Figure 29 is a photograph of saucer-like hollows; when it is viewed upside down, the hollows appear to be convex. This often becomes a problem in architecture. Ornaments, designs, sculpture, done in cameo or intaglio may appear the reverse under different lighting conditions.

The perception of forms in space definitely relates to human interpretation. As Katz states, "All visual percepts are influenced by knowledge that comes from experience." Thus texture (Figure 30), and lineal perspective (Figure 31), offer clues which become more meaningful with age and training. Still other factors operate as guides to the perception of forms in space. These will be discussed in later chapters. They include knowledge of size, apparent movement or motion, the superimposition of one thing upon or in front of another, aerial perspective, comparative brightness, contrast, color purity, and sharpness of detail—as well as the muscular efforts of the eyes at accommodation and convergence.

Finally, perception (including feeling, emotion and a sense of beauty) are properties of human consciousness. If man is awed by the beauty of nature, it is not that some infinite force has endowed nature with anything other than efficient structure—the charm of such structure is man's blessing alone. If he is a real artist he may derive inspiration from nature, but his greatest achievements will come from within the sanctuaries of his own being.

It is necessary to credit man with intelligence and imagination. He does not need to see things carried down to the last detail. Give him mere hints in patterns, designs, color impressions, and he will add the magic of perception. Understanding of Gestalt principles will make possible a truly new art and give the artist new "tools" of expression—tools that are in his own consciousness.

Figure 30. Texture will give clues to distance.

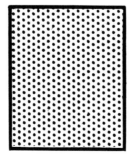

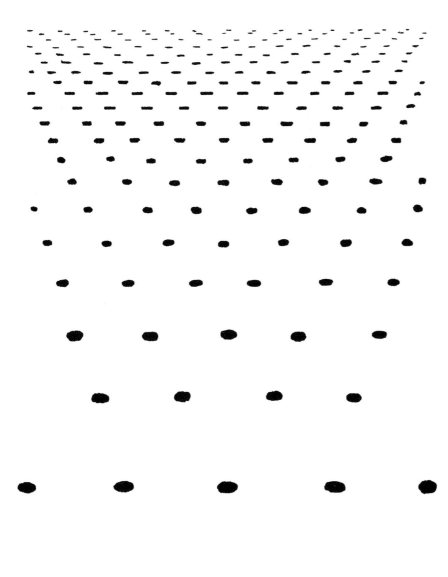

Figure 31. The effect of perspective on a flat plane. After Gibson.

2.

Some Anomalies of Seeing

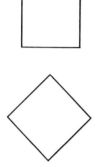

Figure 32. The square at the top appears stable; the square at the bottom is more dynamic.

This chapter will continue the discussion of Gestalt findings—many of which have practical application to three-dimensional form and design.

A number of classical illusions are shown in Plates I and II. Many have been reproduced before and may be familiar. Others are original in concept. However, they all illustrate the strange and remarkable workings of the visual process.

Vernon writes, "A formless percept is unthinkable, and it is impossible to perceive something formless, should such ever occur." Indeed, even the universe itself cannot be conceived as endless. Darkness and "emptiness" themselves seem to have dimension.

As has been said, simplest forms are the easiest to perceive. Yet in perception, the same form may be given different interpretation. Look at Figure 32. Why does a square placed on one of its sides look different from a square balanced on one of its corners? The answer perhaps lies in the fact that one position is stable and the other more dynamic.

Now look at Figure 33, redrawn from Arnheim. If you look at the center figure in relation to the page of this book and the room surrounding, it will appear diamond-like. If you view it in relation to the rectangle that lies about it, the figure will appear as a square.

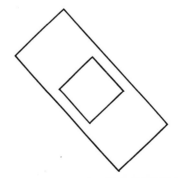

Figure 33. A diamond is seen in relation to the page; a square in relation to the rectangle. After Arnheim.

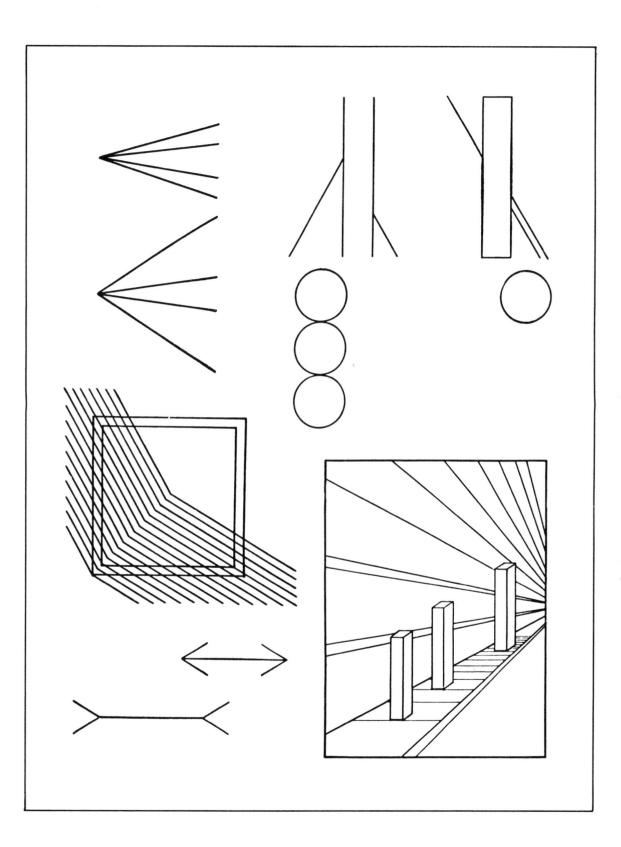

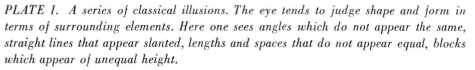

PLATE 1. *A series of classical illusions. The eye tends to judge shape and form in terms of surrounding elements. Here one sees angles which do not appear the same, straight lines that appear slanted, lengths and spaces that do not appear equal, blocks which appear of unequal height.*

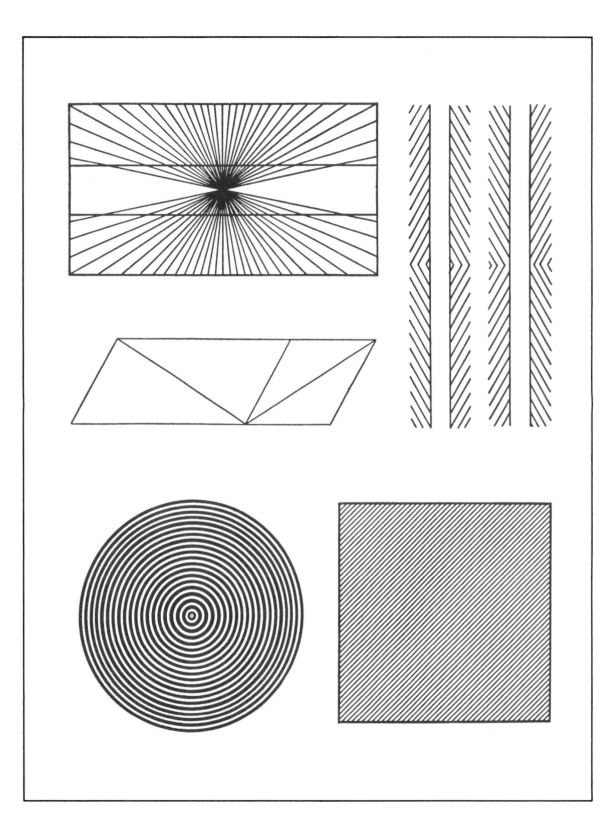

PLATE II. More visual illusions. There are lines that appear to bend, lines that appear unequal in length. In the lower two, steady concentration of the eyes will produce sensation of movement and flecks of subtle color. These also have interesting afterimages.

PLATE III. *A montage showing different modes of appearance for color. In addition to the quality of hue, there can be filminess, structure and solidity, volume or three dimensions, luminosity, luster, iridescence, transparency, plus many other aspects. All of these add further quality to the color impression. (See page 41.)*

Figure 34. Perception seeks meaning in what the eye sees.

In Figure 34, the forms to the left give the mere impression of a group comprising a crescent, a triangle and two circles. If the same designs are turned around, one sees a face. Perception not only tries to simplify what is seen, but it strives to give meaning to it. According to F. C. Bartlett, "The experiments (in perceiving) repeatedly demonstrates that temperament, interest, and attitudes often direct the course and determine the content of perceiving."

The influence of mind and experience account for numerous phenomena which the Gestalt psychologist has studied and revealed to the great benefit of the plastic arts.

For example, forms seen in the upper part of the visual field tend to look relatively smaller and heavier than in the lower part. Distances as well are likely to seem shorter in the sky than on the earth. Several investigators (H. Wölfflin, R. L. Reid) have noted certain left-to-right tendencies in perception. In studies of eye movements, most persons will be found to look from left to right (perhaps because of reading habit). Where such eye movement

Figure 35. There are left-to-right tendencies in vision. A and C look better than B and D.

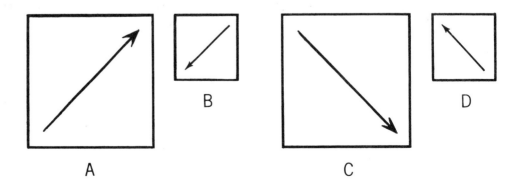

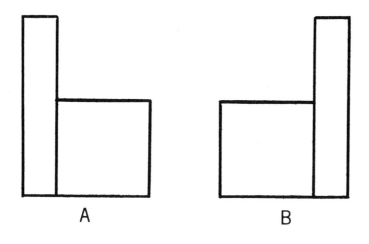

Figure 36. Left (A) is generally stronger than right (B).

is on the diagonal, the direction from bottom left to top right is more natural than the other way around. (See Figure 35.) Similarly, the direction from top left to bottom right is the easier and simpler. Thus in Figure 35, A is better than B, and C is better than D. The same tendencies have been noted when blindfolded subjects have been asked to draw lines. To quote from a review of Reid's work, "These findings open interesting possibilities for research in the psychophysics of esthetics—picture composition, advertising copy, architecture, sculpture; what is the order of eye movement in exploration and why are otherwise pleasing pictures unsatisfactory when reviewed right to left?"

If Reid's findings hold true generally, the arrangement of architectural forms shown in A of Figure 36 would be better than that shown in B. In the theater, it is well known that the left side of the stage is "stronger" than the right.

In Figure 37, man's love of stability and alignment with the forces of gravity will lead a person to see a vertical and horizontal cross rather than a

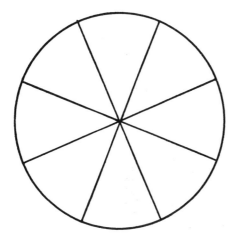

Figure 37. The vertical-horizontal cross will be more persistent than the diagonal one.

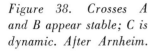

Figure 38. Crosses A and B appear stable; C is dynamic. After Arnheim.

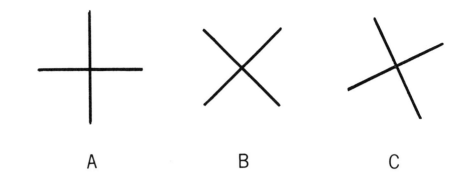

A   B   C

diagonal one, for this is the simpler and more direct of the two. In Figure 38 (after Arnheim), the vertical and diagonal crosses (A and B) look static, while the third one (C) seems in motion; it is off balance. So may forms and shapes be made to appear stable or dynamic.

As has been mentioned, the eye (and perception) struggles to put meaning into whatever it sees. The ancients saw animal figures in the constellations, tracing lines from star to star in rather fanciful outlines. To a small child, pictures may consist of separate scraps—which, incidentally, may be viewed from any angle. Later these scraps become objects, and still later they assume coherence in a meaningful composition.

The eye tends to grasp separate elements into units which are as few in number as possible. It will take apparent chaos (as in Figure 39) and trace paths, organize geometric designs and patterns, and otherwise take action.

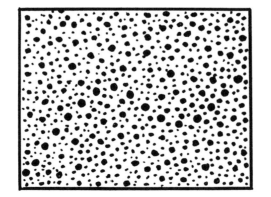

Figure 39. There is action in vision. The eye seeks direction, form or meaning, even in chaos.

And more than this, Köhler discovered that in perception general relationships are more easily remembered than static or fixed qualities. If the reader will recall a few friends, he perhaps will be better able to visualize their general appearance, weight, size, and shape than some specific detail such as which side they part their hair on. Man apparently has a primitive need to grasp the significance of wholes; details are of secondary importance.

Let us turn now to Gestalt factors in color perception; we will relate them to concepts of shape and form in later chapters.

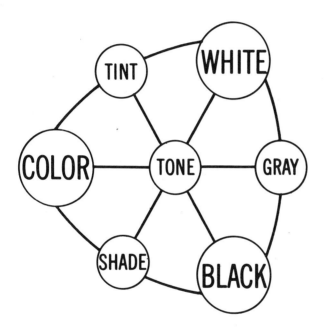

Figure 40. The Color Triangle. All visual sensations are classified in terms of these seven "boxes."

Study the Color Triangle, shown in Figure 40. The psychologist, Ewald Hering, was first to point out that the natural symbol of color was a triangle, with pure hue (red, yellow, green, blue, etc.) on one angle, white on the second, and black on the third. He was also first to establish the truth that all color variations in perceptions were derived from these three elements.

Remember that these statements concern color as *sensation,* not as radiant energy. In physics, black is negative. Three primary light sources or filters (red, green, blue-violet) combined with white light are all that are necessary in physical color measurement. But in vision, black is definitely positive, a precise and fundamental sensation and not like "nothingness."

Now these three primary forms—pure color, white, black—have four simple derivatives. Pure color and white combine to form tint. Pure color and black combine to form shade. White and black combine to form gray. The final form, tone, is the product of all: color, white and black; or tint, shade and gray.

In a broad sense, and chiefly as related to so-called surface color, this is all there is to color perception. Every visual sensation may be classified as one of these seven forms. Pure colors are unique as sensations and do not look like white or black. The same uniqueness exists for white and for black. However, the secondary forms (tint, shade, tone, gray), resemble the primary forms that compose them.

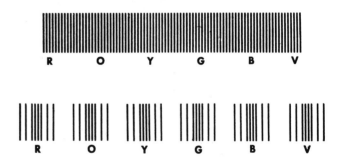

Figure 41. The eye tends to see individual colors in the spectrum, not continuous gradations.

As to pure colors, while red, green, blue-violet are primary in light (additive color), and red, yellow, blue are primary in pigments (subtractive color), in the psychology of vision, the primaries are four in number: red, yellow, green and blue. These also are unique. For example, while yellow and green hardly resemble each other, yellow-green resembles both.

In looking at a complete spectrum (see Figure 41), the eye will do its best to reduce the number of colors it sees to a minimum. Although the spectrum contains innumerable wave lengths, each of which is distinct from the stand-point of physics, in vision there is evident simplification. Instead of seeing countless gradations, the colors are bunched together as sensations. Newton saw these as red, yellow, green, blue, indigo and violet. Today the grouping usually omits indigo.

Indeed, in pure spectral light there are not as many colors as most people suppose. After studying the matter, Selig Hecht wrote, "The normal eye can separate the visible spectrum with complete certainty into about 180 patches of hues which cannot be made to look like one another by varying their intensities."

Spectral light, of course, is pure, and does not involve color mixtures and variations associated with the addition of black and gray. And even here, simplification takes place. To speak of millions of colors is specious and psychologically untrue. It is quite probable that not more than 10,000 *different* colors and color variations could be assembled in painted or dyed samples. To see even this many would require plenty of light and very ideal seeing conditions.

Remember that although the world of color may be infinite and complex, human consciousness does its best to work toward simplification. The Color Triangle of Figure 40 is a shining example. Color constancy, to be discussed later, is another. Briefly, it is human for the eye (and brain) to function in simple ways: to take the innumerable wave lengths of the spectrum and bunch them together into few rather than countless hue sensations; to respond to millions of intermediate color modifications and yet to put them in the seven boxes of Figure 40; to hold recognition and constancy for "genuine" color under radically different conditions of illumination and environment.

Here are some human facts that offer lessons for architects and designers in the harmony of color and form—all paying tribute to the Gestalt of seeing.

—Just as the eye has best perception for simple forms (circles, squares, triangles, rectangles), so does it see greatest elementary beauty in simple colors, red, yellow, green, blue, (black and white). These are difficult to surpass where mass appeal is concerned. Chapter 4 will discuss and illustrate different "palettes" for use by architects and designers. As a rule, primary colors are strong in impulse and have universal appeal; intermediate colors are more subtle and perhaps for this reason more livable.

—A natural preference for simplicity and preciseness further teaches that colors, when pure, should be unmistakably so. When modified, they should be made into distinct and clear-cut examples of tint, shade, gray, tone. Avoid

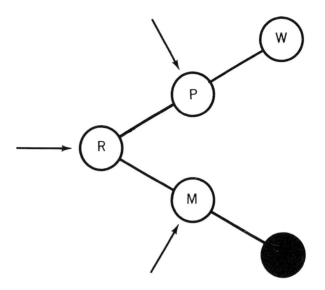

Figure 42. Precise "form" is preferred in color. Borderline variations are not as pleasant as well-spaced intervals.

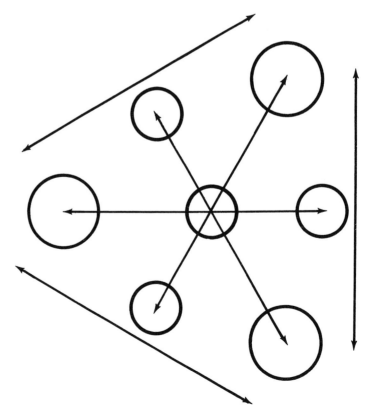

Figure 43. These are natural and harmonious paths in color sequence.

borderline indecisions. People generally do not respond freely to what is vague or uncertain in perception. (See Figure 42.)

—The Color Triangle of Figure 40 not only charts the seven basic forms of color, but it indicates harmonious paths or sequences. Trace lines in any straight direction and the color forms are visually and psychologically related. Consequently, any such scales are beautiful. (See Figure 43.)

—The most neutral of all forms is the tone, not gray, for it blends hue with white and black. In large architectural mass, toned colors (particularly cool ones such as soft blues, blue-greens and greens) make the best of all ground

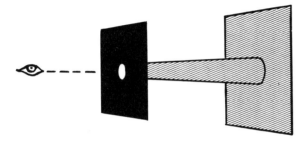

Figure 44. Surface colors may appear like film colors if viewed through an aperture screen.

colors and will combine ideally and effectively with practically any and all other color forms. This point will be elaborated in Chapter 4.

But colors in the perceptual sense also have what are called different modes of appearance. (See Plate III.) Here there may be remarkable independence between the facts of visual stimulation and the human interpretation of them. Wilhelm Ostwald noted the difference between "film" colors and "surface" colors, a vital distinction indeed and one that was overlooked by such great scientists as Helmholtz. Film color is light, so to speak—with black excluded. It is the color of space, seen in the open sky, without contrasting horizon effects, and in spectrometers. It generally is unrelated to an environment. Film colors for the most part contain no apparent black. An orange light bulb, controlled by a rheostat in a dark room, will remain orange, whether light or dim. Surface colors, on the other hand, are definitely structural and localized. They are the colors revealed by and part of an environment. And they usually contain black. Orange paint, modified by black paint, no longer is orange but brown, a different perceptual experience.

Surface colors, incidentally, may be turned to the aspect of film colors by viewing them through an aperture screen. (See Figure 44.) The surface color, of course, must be without decided texture. Another demonstration of the film color, devised by Katz, is to hold a card midway toward a page. If the card is held so that it cuts off the vision of one eye—and if it is jiggled slightly—a person may sense the existence of a soft gray film between the eye and the page.

David Katz has described other modes of appearance. If film colors seem to fill infinite space, and if surface colors are localized, volume colors lie intermediate. Fog, for example, will be like a film color until objects are seen through it; then it will resemble volume color—that is, it will seem to occupy definite space. Refer to Plate III. It is theoretically conceivable that one particular color (red) might appear filmy like a patch of sunset sky; that it might be hard and structural; that it might be three-dimensional; and further that it might be luminous, lustrous, iridescent, transparent, metallic, plain, thickly textured, etc. Although a scientific instrument might record one and the same red energy in all instances, there would be a world of difference in human experience.

In terms of architecture and three-dimensional form, these effects are most compelling and will be discussed in later chapters. Once these phenomena of vision are understood, they may be readily simulated in controlled illusion, thus enhancing artistic expression. See *Creative Color* for a discussion of color effects in painting and two-dimensional design.

The spectrum may be divided into warm colors (red, orange, yellow), and cool colors (green, blue, violet), with yellow-green and red-violet occupying more or less "neutral" positions. The eminent French color theorist, M. E. Chevreul, used the terms luminous for the warm and somber for the cool. Another description might be advancing and receding colors. Goethe spoke of positive and active colors for the warm ones, and negative and passive colors for the cool ones.

However, the Gestalt psychologist speaks of *hard* and *soft* colors and has good reason for doing so. In an investigation by S. Liebmann (described by Koffka), it has been found that brightness difference is more important than hue difference in the discrimination of areas or patterns on grounds. For example, a gray figure on a slightly deeper gray ground will have a more "stable organization" than a deeply saturated blue figure on a gray ground of the same brightness or value. Koffka writes, "This proves that difference of stimulation is not in itself equivalent to segregation of area." (See A in Plate IV.)

However, not all colors are alike in this respect. Where grays of equal

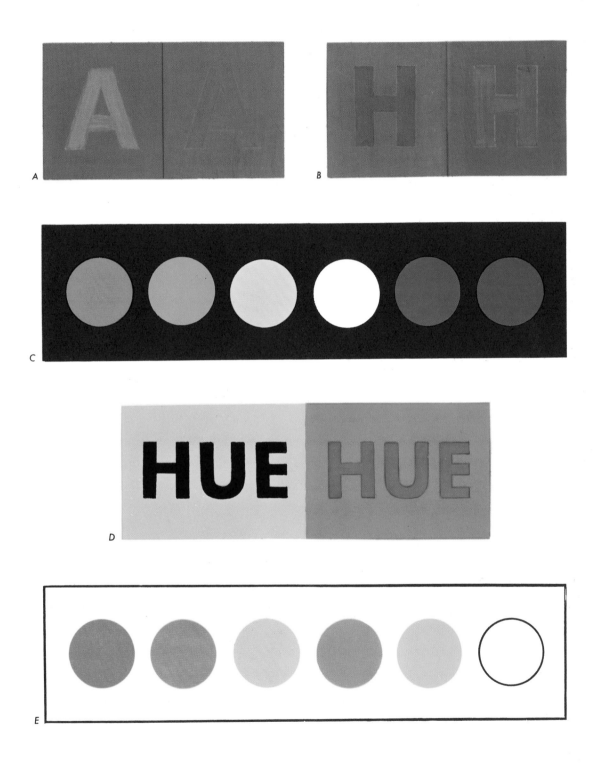

PLATE IV. The effects shown concern "hard" colors (A); "soft" colors (B); visibility of colors (C); legibility (D); attention-power (E).

luminosity (value or brightness) are combined with hued figures, red and orange will "segregate" the best; and blue and green will "segregate" the poorest. Therefore, the former are *hard* colors and the latter are *soft*. (White will similarly be hard, while black will be soft.) Also pertinent is the fact that colors "articulate" better against gray when they are on the figure rather than on the background. (See B in Plate IV.) This is especially true of hard colors (red, orange). According to Koffka, red letters on a gray ground can be seen at a greater distance than gray letters on a red ground.

In color fusion, it will be found that the hard colors (red, orange) will dominate the soft colors (blue, green). If a red card is exposed to one eye and a blue card to the other eye (simultaneously), perfect fusion in the center of the brain will result in a mixture of the two (a purple). However, *before* fusion takes place, the brain will persist in seeing red more often and for larger periods than it will see blue. White here will also be dominant over black.

Let us consider some facts about seeing—facts that have many practical applications to the color problems of architects and designers.

First of all, visual acuity. The eye has different sensitivity under different conditions of illumination. In the light-adapted eye, the spectrum is brightest at yellow and yellow-green. In the dark-adapted eye, the spectrum is brightest at blue-green, and red may fade out into blackness. (See Figure 45.)

Figure 45. Yellow and yellow-green have highest visibility in daylight. The point of highest visibility at night is blue-green.

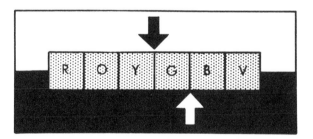

Regarding colored light sources, M. Luckiesh points out that yellow is the region of maximum selectivity, the brightest region of the spectrum. It is without aberration (that is, the eye normally focuses it sharply) and it is fairly pleasing psychologically. Luckiesh has demonstrated that by filtering out blue and violet radiation in a mercury light (or tungsten filament) visual acuity remained practically constant, despite the reduced amount of light absorbed by the filter. As far as acuity is concerned, this would mean that yellow has some advantages. Sodium vapor illumination, for example, is highly efficient—although its distortion of surface colors makes it impossible for use if good appearance in the environment is necessary.

Two authorities, Ferree and Rand, place yellow illumination at the top of the list for good visibility, orange-yellow second, followed by yellow-green and green. Deep red, blue and violet are least desirable. Blue light, in fact, is very difficult for the eye to focus and will cause objects to appear blurred and surrounded by halos.

Under extreme dark adaptation, however, the eye seems to have excellent acuity for red light—and such illumination is used in airplanes, ships and control rooms where good seeing under dim conditions is required. Red light does not seem to disturb dark-adaptation. In fact, the wearing of red goggles or eyeshades in daylight will effectively condition the eye for good darkness visibility.

As to point light sources seen in distance, simple visibility and recognition may be two different things. That is, while white light may carry well through distance, the eye may find some difficulty in locating it. Granted that the brighter the source, the easier and farther it will be seen, red is perhaps best and first. It is instantly recognized and plainly visible, even at low intensities. Green is second, yellow third, and white fourth. Blue and purple become hopelessly lost to blur in darkness and distance. (See C in Plate IV.)

When surface colors are seen in daylight, however, the color of highest visibility is yellow. Black on yellow is the most legible of all color combinations; it is even superior to black on white in brilliant daylight because yellow is more compelling than white, and also because yellow creates a sharper image on the retina (white may tend to "haze"). Other highly legible combinations, are green on white, red on white, blue on white, white on blue, black on white, white on black. Combinations of red and blue, red and green, or blue and green are poor. (See D in Plate IV.)

In attention-power, red-orange rates first and is superior to yellow. Next are the other hard colors of the psychologist, red, orange, yellow-orange, yellow, pink—plus a luminous yellow-green. In air-sea rescue work the Navy has demonstrated the superiority of red-orange over yellow, white or any other color. Because of its extreme visual impact (richness or chromaticity), it will persist in forcing itself upon human vision and consciousness where other colors, though highly visible, may go unnoticed. (See E in Plate IV.)

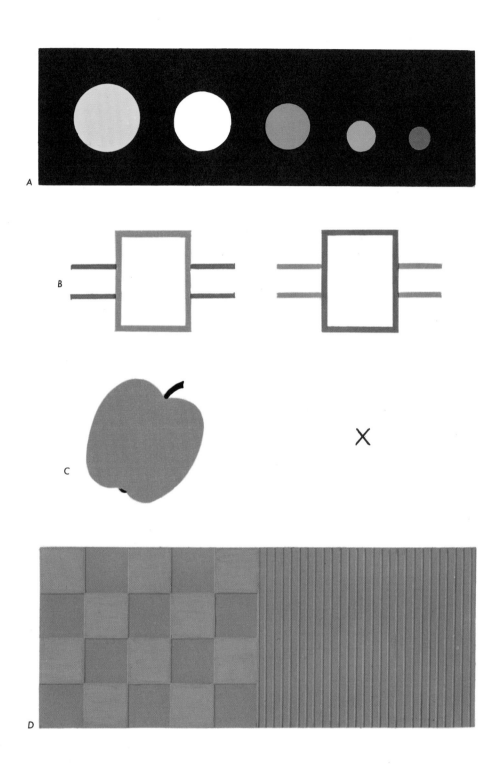

PLATE V. Diagrams show apparent sizes of colors (A), dimension in color (B), the afterimage (C), the juxtaposition and diffusion of colors (D).

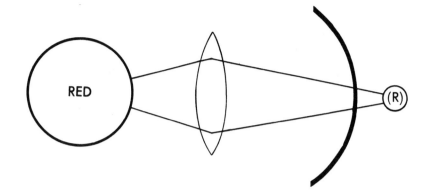

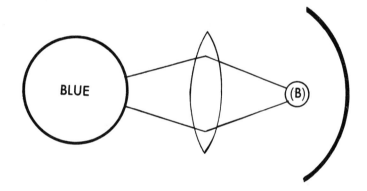

Figure 46. The focus of the eye to red and blue.

Because the focus of the human eye is not the same for all hues, different colors appear near or far, large or small. (See Figure 46.) In general, size and apparent distance involve similar functions in vision. Thus yellow will be seen as the nearest and largest of colors, white next, then red, green, blue and black. This order will hold true in full daylight and may even defy judgments based on perspective, visual orientation and depth perception. (See A in Plate V.)

However, dimension is also related to aerial perspective and the effects of atmosphere and mist. These matters will be taken up in later chapters.

In the perspective of color, warm and light colors should generally be designed to appear in front of cool and deep colors. (See B in Plate V.)

However, distance is gray, not black. In Figure 47, gray forms recede from white (which is near) into light, medium and deep grays. The swing is then back forward again to black. White and black, to be seen distinctly as such, require strong light and nearness to the eye. Their "genuine" qualities suffer as illumination grows dim or as forms of them retreat into distance.

Much will be said and illustrated in this book about color, space and the influence of illumination and atmosphere. These are more important to perspective than the different focal points of warm and cold colors. In fact, *all* pure colors in a sense look near, because only in such position is their intensity clearly seen. Conversely, *all* gray colors look distant, for perception associates grayness with things afar. However, there are qualifications to these general statements which will be presented in the chapters on illumination and color constancy.

Various color illusions and phenomena are illustrated and described in Plates IV and V. Afterimages (C in Plate V), while interesting, do not play much of a role in average seeing. Hence they are deserving of academic attention only. It is by no means normal for people to sit and stare at anything; typical perception is marked by continual eye movements and shifts in visual, mental, and emotional direction.

Effects of contrast in brightness are worthy of mention. Many books on color show the influence of colors upon each other. This, as mentioned, requires steady concentration, and is rarely granted by average viewers of color arrangements. Effects of brightness contrast, on the other hand, are noticeable on sight.

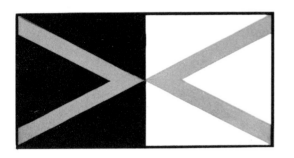

Figure 48. Brightness con-
trast. Both gray arrows
are the same.

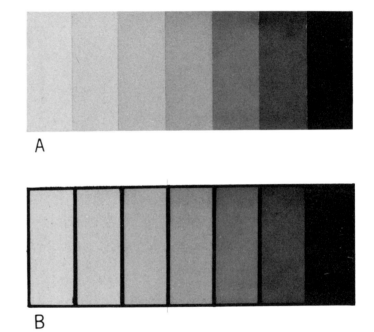

A

Figure 49. Fluting effects
caused by brightness con-
trast can be corrected by
black outlines.

B

Look at Figure 48. Both arrows are the same light gray. To the left, the arrow looks light, while to the right it looks dark. In vision, when light and dark areas are placed side by side, the dark area will make the adjacent light area appear brighter, and the light area will make the adjacent dark area appear deeper—at one and the same time.

This may often result in a fluting effect, as demonstrated in Figure 49. In the seven steps of the top scale (A), each band is uniform and flat; yet they all appear shaded. The illusion may happen quite frequently where color schemes are so arranged in bands or stripes, and designers and architects would do well to bear it in mind. If the fluting is to be eliminated, this may be done by separating the areas or giving them a white or black outline, as in B of Figure 49.

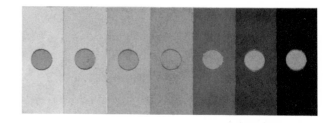

Figure 50. The center gray spots are the same throughout. Note apparent change in value. After Hering.

In Figure 50 is a classical illusion devised by the eminent psychologist, Ewald Hering. In the center of a seven-step gray scale, one identical spot of light gray appears to be anything but uniform. These spots, indeed, seem to scale from dark to light in inverse order to the scale itself.

Colors have weight, and a sense of weight refers automatically to a sense of right and proper sequence. Study the arrangements of forms in Figure 51. Colors appear heavy or light depending on whether they are low or high in value. Yellow is a lighter color (by apparent weight) than blue. Hence, A in Figure 51 appears well-balanced. Arrangement B is less so, but still in agreeable sequence (and more like inverted typographical than architectural balance). C and D arrangements are not satisfactory, the distribution of weight being far from convincing. However, in Figure 52, if weight is adjusted to mass, so to speak, the C sequence in Figure 51 may be satisfactorily "engineered." Here gray at the base, white in the center, and black at the top are neatly balanced (mass as against weight), and the result is visually pleasing. It takes good training, insight and judgment on the part of the architect or designer to handle color weight. Neglect of it may often result in effects that look distressing to average observers.

Figure 53 illustrates a point about color and area which is highly significant to the appearance of areas and forms seen from a distance. There is a

Figure 51. The eye prefers neat sequence in color value or weight.

A

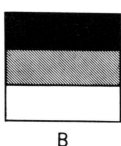

B

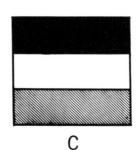

C

D

traditional rule that pure colors ought to be in small centralized areas and modified colors in large background areas. Also, warmth is best for the feature and coolness for the foil. This may be academic, but it is fairly good advice. However, it is even more important to consider area relationships.

To begin with, it would be distressing to arrange alternate areas of pure red and blue in bands, patterns or designs. The two colors cannot be focused simultaneously. The result would be unpleasant if the areas were fairly large, or a vibrant purple if the areas were small and diffused in vision.

While black and white are used in Figure 53, the principle involved applies also to colors, and an example is given in D of Plate V. When two contrasting colors are isolated in large areas, their differences will be distinct and they will stand out in bold contrast, as on the left side of Figure 53. When, however, the contrasting colors are arranged in fine lines or dots and when the eye is forced to blend or confuse them, contrast is lost and the hues will cancel each other, as on the right of Figure 53 where white and black have become gray.

Thus when colors are *isolated*, the stronger the contrast (in hue or brightness or both), the *stronger* the effect.

When colors are *diffused* in the eye, the stronger the contrast, the *weaker* the effect.

On the other hand, if the colors involved are analogous or related, an opposite result may be expected.

Colors that are similar in hue or brightness, when isolated, will lack contrast.

Colors similar in hue, when diffused, may, through optical mixture, appear to be increased in vividness.

For example, red and green, when isolated, will appear quite garish. When diffused, they will cancel into a muddy brown.

Red and violet, when isolated, will be bright enough but more or less flat. When diffused, they may become a shimmering purple.

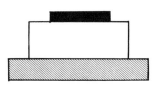

Figure 52. Adjustment of apparent weight to mass.

Figure 53. The juxtaposition and diffusion of colors.

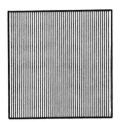

3.

The Apparent Colors of Form

The psychologist has pretty well substantiated the fact that color is more elemental and primitive than form in human perception. As a matter of fact, response to form seems to arouse mental (judgment of shape) or physical (touch) processes, while reactions to color are more impulsive and emotional.

In writing of the Rorschach method, M. Rickers-Ousiankina states, "Color experience when it occurs, is thus a much more immediate and direct sense datum than the experience of form. Form perception is usually accompanied by a detached, objective attitude in the subject. Whereas the experience of color, being more immediate, is likely to contain personal, affectively toned notes."

Children may be color "dominant," while adults may be form "dominant." David Katz writes, "Color, rather than shape, is more closely related to emotion."

To demonstrate this, he devised the experiment shown in Figure 54. A child is given a red triangle (to the left of the line, indicated by black), and asked to match it against other colors and forms in other shapes. Although the test is ambiguous (there is only *one* red triangle, for example), Katz found that "as a rule younger children choose a form of similar color rather than similar shape." In other words, color is what attracts, and form is incidental. Writes Katz, "This finding confirms the primacy of color in creating form." He goes on to say, "In reporting this finding for the first time a number of years ago, the writer sought to explain it on a basis of the stronger

Figure 54. Experiment devised by Katz. Colors are easier to relate than forms.

PLATE VI. (Top) Model of spray-form house. John MacL. Johansen, Architect. Photograph: E. J. Cyr. (Bottom) The Solomon R. Guggenheim Museum, New York City. Frank Lloyd Wright, Architect. (See page 70.)

PLATE VII. (Top) Zarauela Hippodrome, Madrid. Eduardo Torroja, Architect.
Photograph: M. Garcia Moya. (Bottom) Model of TWA Terminal, Idlewild Airport.
Eero Saarinen and Associates, Architects. (See page 70.)

PLATE VIII. (Top) Restaurant, Xochimilco. Joaquin and Fernando Ordonez, Architectural Designers. Cubiertas Ala, S.A., Engineers. (Bottom) Congress Hall, Berlin. Hugh Stubbins and Associates, Architects. (See page 70.)

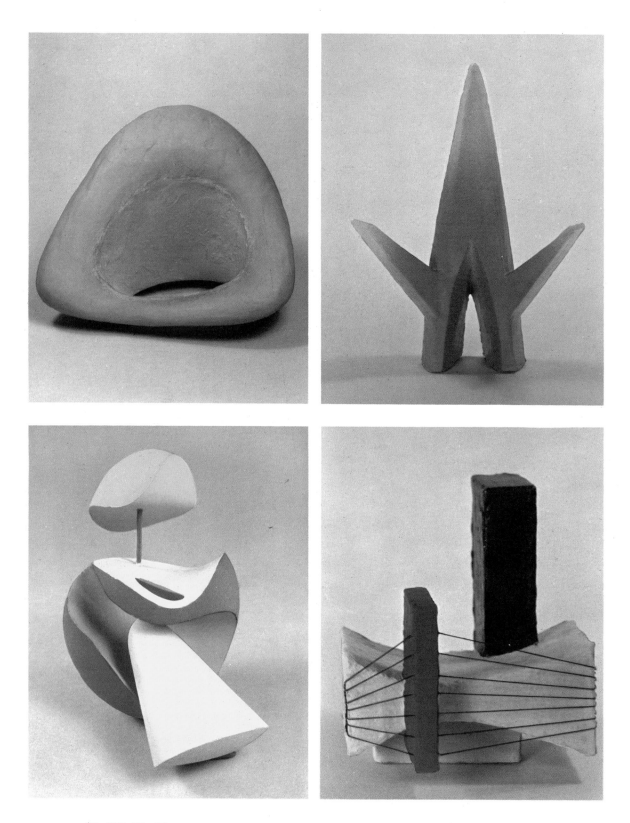

PLATE IX. Physiognomic perception as expressed in four plastic models. Here the artist has tried to relate the spirit of color to the spirit of form. The interpretation, of course, is personal and offers engaging possibilities to creative minds. Upper left is meant to appear homelike; upper right, spiritual. Lower left is a blithe form; and lower right, a practical form. (See page 70.)

coherence of identically colored forms. It could also be explained from the standpoint of Gestalt theory by pointing out that *color is more important than shape in the creation of forms."*

An adult, faced with the problem of Figure 54, would point out the discrepancies of color and form and perhaps hesitate—or ask what is to be matched, shape or color? However, if the shapes are only momentarily exposed, adults "follow the children's example and choose a similar object on the basis of similar color."

In theory, at least, it would seem that any three-dimensional creation of the architect or designer ought to begin with color first and form second! This is a radical concept, of course. But if color is so immediate in human experience, why shouldn't its impression, its visual and emotional qualities, be the first of all considerations?

All too often color is looked upon as something esthetic and emotional, a sort of frill to vision. One may forget that the sense of color is quite primitive and was given to man by nature to aid his acuity, orient him better to the world, and contribute to his survival. Surely, man does not see color in order to admire sunsets, flowers and works of art.

Yet cultural interpretations have frequently been interjected. Sophisticated persons have attributed to the spectrum, qualities which it does not possess, and to man responses which are wholly superficial. Color comes before form, not after. It is far more basic in perception.

To pursue the idea, let it be assumed that an architect is to design a home, a church, a theater, an office building. Surely, each of these could be given a basic mood, meaning or purpose, which could be expressed with color just as well as with design. It doesn't take much imagination to get a feeling for color and to decide that particular colors are "homelike," "spiritual," "gay and diverting," or "functional and efficient." Suppose the project began here. The artist at least would start out trying to convey an impression which the public would undoubtedly recognize. Even more important, his primary acceptance of color would influence his thoughts about design and form— for all are related. He might be able to create a final unity of result that would be beautiful because it had Gestalt factors as well as factors of reason in its concept!

Color associations are also primitive. The symbolism attached to red will be found to have the virile qualities of fire, blood and the strong visual impact of the hue itself. The symbolism of blue will relate to water, sky and the physically calming effects of the hue.

If there is anything to so-called color psychology, it traces directly to the fact that visual and physiological processes are activated by warm (hard) colors and retarded by cool (soft) colors. This is where man gets his notions about color—from the reactions of his body which prod the fancies of his mind.

The author is sure he will be forgiven for his defense of color. It is not a thing apart, a superfluity or adornment. It is not something to come *after* form: it should truly come *before*, or at least at the *same time*. Many of the structures of antiquity seem to have been conceived simultaneously in terms of color and form. The monuments of Egypt, the ziggurats of Asia Minor, the temples of Greece were all colored—if not on a basis of Gestalt, then because of symbolism and metaphysics which in turn were derived from deep-set responses. This historical story has been told in the author's *New Horizons in Color,* and will be mentioned only briefly here and in the next chapter.

The western prejudice against color (which is breaking down) constitutes a sort of Freudian trauma born of Puritanism. Frank Lloyd Wright was once moved to call the Greeks "the original interior desecrators." As if the Greek could be a boor with hue while a superman with form! And the mighty Rodin, who found out about the use of color in Greek polychrome reliefs, is said to have struck his breast and muttered, "I feel it here that these were never colored." But colored they were, and by no means timidly. In his engaging book, *Gods, Graves and Scholars,* C. W. Ceram writes, "The plastic works of the ancient Greeks were gaily colored. Statuary was deeply dyed with garish pigments. The marble figure of a woman found in the Athenian Acropolis was tinctured red, green, blue, and yellow. Quite often statues had red lips, glowing eyes made of precious stones, and even artificial eyelashes."

As has been said earlier, color cannot be divorced from form. Any such attempts are doomed to failure and run contrary to the whole reality of life. All too often the architect and designer assume that gray form is colorless form, and that the choice is between form (gray) and color. This cannot possibly be. There are no models of "colorlessness" in nature. What is the answer to the most basic question of all: Why does man have color vision?

To hear many a purist expound, one would think that man's sense of color is somehow artificial and civilized. The color sense is as old as man himself. It is not of recent origin as are many existing concepts of form. If anyone looks upon color as something akin to affectation, he is totally wrong. Man responded to color long before he had the slightest notion about shapes, proportions, parabolic curves and the whole kit of esthetic conventions which culture has assigned to what is called art and beauty today.

When Pythagoras related his solids to the elements and to colors (Figure 1), he was concerned with metaphysics, not perception. It is probably true that many artists of the past saw forms as colors and colors as forms, although many such interpretations were usually personal. In ancient symbolism, when red was related to fire (heat, blood, sacrifice), yellow to the sun (light, wisdom), blue to coldness (air, water, truth), green to nature (life everlasting), a sort of psychological or spiritual kinship was recognized. In truth, the symbolic meanings attached to colors over the centuries have not been altogether arbitrary, but have followed moods and feelings prompted by visual and physiological responses.

In Christian mysticism, for example, heaven was blue, earth yellow and hell red—quite understandably. The Heavenly Trinity (Figure 55) was often portrayed with blue for God the Father, yellow for God the Son, and red for God the Holy Ghost. Quite similarly, man had three aspects to his nature, his body symbolized by red, his mind by yellow and his spirit by blue.

Figure 55. Medieval conception of the Trinity.

In heraldry, red is for courage and zeal, gold or yellow for honor and loyalty, green for youth and hope, blue for truth and sincerity, purple for royalty and rank, silver or white for faith and purity, and black for grief and penitence.

A more intelligible alliance with perception began to arise as man gave more attention to the actual visual and physiological effects of color. Edwin D. Babbitt, a "miracle healer" and mystic of the past century, gave blue the form of the circle, yellow the hexagon, and red the triangle. To him the circle, having no corners, represented the spaciousness and tranquility of blue. The triangle, sturdy and with sharp angles, expressed the energy of red. The hexagon, neither round nor angular, partook of both the calmness and vitality of yellow.

A fairly reasonable association between color and form is presented in Figure 56. While these were devised by the author, similar associations were noted by the abstract painter, Kandinsky.

As shown in Figure 46, because the eye focused differently to different colors (farsighted for red, nearsighted for blue), warm colors appear larger than cool colors. At the same time, red, orange and yellow form sharp and clear images on the retina, while the images of blue and violet tend to be blurred. Thus colors assume shapes and forms as follows. Emotional impressions, however, are incidental; these are the ways colors seem to "look" rather than "feel."

Red suggests the form of the square or cube. It is hot, dry and opaque in quality. It is heavy, solid and substantial and holds a strong visual attraction. Because it is sharply focused by the eye, it lends itself to structural planes and sharp angles.

Orange suggests the rectangle. It is less earthly in quality than red, rising higher and being tinged with incandescence. It is warm, dry, compelling. Optically it produces a sharp image and therefore lends itself to angles and to well defined ornament.

Yellow suggests the form of the triangle or pyramid with its point or apex down. It is the color of highest visibility in the spectrum and therefore sharp, angular and crisp in quality. Yet it does not have much weight; it is more like light than substance, more spatial than solid.

Green suggests the form of the hexagon or icosahedron. It is cool, fresh, spacious. It is not sharply focused and therefore does not lend itself to much angularity. Because of its association with nature, green is a big color and can dominate the eye without distressing it.

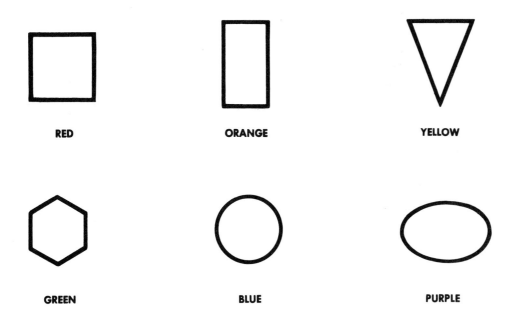

RED ORANGE YELLOW

GREEN BLUE PURPLE

Figure 56. The apparent shapes or forms of colors.

Blue suggests the form of the circle or sphere. It is cold, wet, transparent, atmospheric. It is further retiring, is poorly focused in vision and usually creates a blurred image on the retina—particularly from a distance. While it may have bulk, it does not lend itself to sharpness or detail.

Purple suggests the form of the oval. It is somewhat more refined than blue, and the eye also finds difficulty in focusing it. Purple is soft, filmy and never angular. Unlike blue however, it is not so infinite or spacious but clings to earth like the distant mountain half hidden in mist.

The author's *New Horizons in Color* repeats the above analogies between color and form and then proceeds to the fascinating subject of physiognomic perception. Since then (1955) a study of the phenomenon has been continued; it is undoubtedly one of the most fertile of all fields for architects and those who design in three dimensions, for it deals with the Gestalt of seeing in a most esthetic as well as practical way.

The term physiognomic perception was devised by Heinz Werner, and his book, *Comparative Psychology of Mental Development,* is highly recommended. Man sees the world in a dynamic rather than static way. The "pictures" which his eye projects on his brain are not like mere photographs in an album. On the contrary, the brain works on these "pictures" and adds much to them. They take on meaning that is affected and influenced by his whole emotional and psychic makeup.

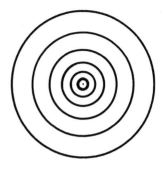

Figure 57. The dynamic qualities of fire and water expressed in line. After Bragdon.

Figure 58. Which is "takete" and which is "maluma"? After Köhler.

Accompanying illustrations are pertinent. In Figure 57, Claude Bragdon expresses the dynamic qualities of fire and water, such associations being rather direct. Köhler developed two nonsense words, "takete" and "maluma" and two abstract patterns shown in Figure 58; he found that virtually all subjects tested agreed as to which word applied to which pattern.

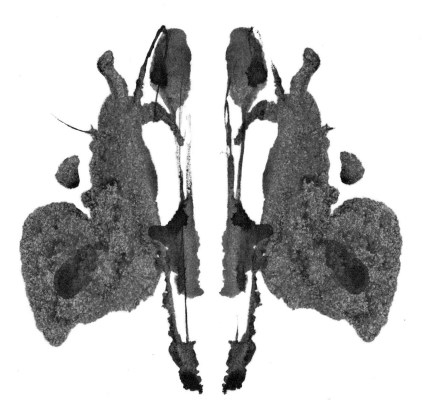

In a sense, the Rorschach test, using ink blots, is related to physiognomic perception. With it the psychologist attempts to arouse thoughts, fancies and images from his patient. (See Figure 59.) Where color is added to the ink blots, the emotionally excited person may react freely and impulsively. The more depressed individual may experience "color shock" and reject the color as an unwanted intrusion on his inner life.

Perception, being a dynamic experience, is less inspired by that which is unmistakably clear and literal than by that which is somewhat vague. Werner writes, "If it is admitted that the things of the child's world are created as much by his motor-affective activity as by objective stimuli, it becomes intelligible, for instance, why a child can seriously consider a few wisps of straw to be a doll or a bit of wood to be a horse. . . . His experience of a doll does not need to contain a head with two eyes, a nose, a mouth, and so on."

Arnheim has wisely written, "We are neglecting the gift of comprehending things by what our senses tell us about them. . . . The weaker the artist, the more thoroughly will the illusion of material presence crowd out visually comprehensible meaning."

At times, modern art has been brutally attacked for its crudeness, seeming childishness and "cave man" approach to design and form. In painting, the epitome of all this will perhaps be found in Kasimir Malevich's painting which he called "White on White." It is similar to the sketch shown in Figure 60—a white square on a slightly duller white background—nothing more. Malevich called his art Suprematism and said, "Suprematism is the supremacy of the pure feeling in the plastic arts."

It is only fair to say that this is intellectual exercise rather than art. Mohaly-Nagy wrote of the white on white composition that it was "extremely revealing as a symbol of the transition from painting in terms of pigments to painting in terms of light." Maybe so, but art needs more than words. All too often, too much of it requires the services of a barker to give it sense, if indeed it has sense. This is unfortunate, for it should speak for itself in some intelligible fashion, even if vague.

Life has changed since previous centuries and ancient times. The speed is faster. Man no longer can devote himself to meticulous detail, to craftsmanship that makes uneconomical use of labor. There must be simpler methods and more dynamic and imaginative resourcefulness. If I may add my own criticism, none of this needs to resort to dull splotches and scribblings. Instead of the primitive, art should play upon the senses, exploit the magic of seeing, physiognomic perception; it should inspire human participation. Man can and should out-think the artists of the past, for he has available in Gestalt psychology a comprehension of new design elements of which his predecessors were largely ignorant.

In the physiognomic sense, there is much that is cold, literal, intellectual probably, but hardly fanciful in a lot of architecture, both old and new.

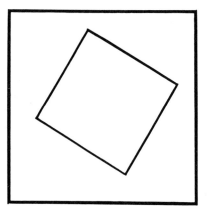

Figure 60. Sketch of "White on White" by Kasimir Malevich.

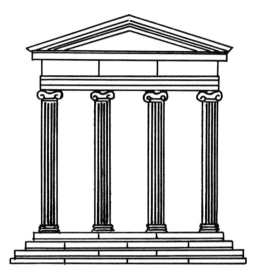

Figure 61. Classical and modern architectural forms.

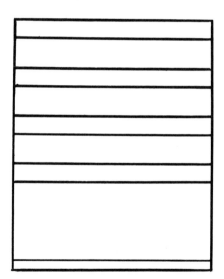

Stripped of its adornments, much of classical tradition was severe and geometrical. And much of modern architecture resembles giant packing cases. (See Figure 61.) Form has often spoken bluntly—like a doll with perfect eyes, nose, mouth. It may have awed and impressed, but it hardly has inspired much participation. It is there before you as the artist and engineer fully intended. But the viewer is little more than a bystander; asked to be witness but not truly invited to take part.

Figure 62. Gothic and oriental architectural forms.

Some Gothic and Oriental forms, on the other hand, were more whimsical. (See Figure 62.) Silhouetted against the sky, they assumed phantasmic shapes that allowed the viewer to let his fancies soar. He could, in fact, imagine saints or demons, as his conscience was moved. His perception could participate. This is rare in modern days, though not wholly unknown, as will be seen later.

What is physiognomic perception? Refer to Figure 63 which shows three physiognomic drawings taken from a special monograph by Reinhard Krauss. More of them and a further discussion will be found in my book, *New Horizons in Color*.

In physiognomic perception there is a "dynamization of things." Perception (and experience) adds to what it sees. The viewer becomes an artist in his own right, in that he takes part in what he views. And the artist is great who can create pleasurable reactions.

It is quite easy for average persons to translate thoughts, feelings and moods into designs and forms. Pointed things may be sharp and cruel. Sagging things may be tired or lazy. Bulging things may be soft and jolly. Tensed will, longing, fury, are physiognomically expressed in Figure 63. The associations could be developed endlessly. What is important is simply this: man has an inherent and dynamic interest in what he beholds. Nature may teach him lessons in beauty, but essentially he has an intuition of his own. The art of the future could well become physiognomic and, in so doing, create forms and effects which would break with and surpass the best traditions of the past. It could be majestically original.

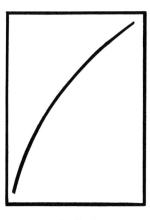

LONGING

FURY

TENSED WILL

Figure 63. Experiments in physiognomic perception.

Figure 64. Forms and meanings do not require full detail.

COLOR

The modern artist has one point to his credit; art and beauty do not have to be complete in all details—completeness may be implied. Let the artist and his public work together in the total and final effort. In Figure 64, the word COLOR is instantly perceived though it lacks neat outline. Here literacy is required, for the markings would be meaningless otherwise. In Figure 65 are well-known symbols of a seagull, star, lightning. A few apparently careless lines are translated by the mind into a man, a face, a horse (or dog). Children are quite adept in reducing complex things to simple elements.

Figure 65. The reduction of things to simple elements or symbols.

Figure 66. Two Droodles.

Figure 67. "Bird in Space," by Brancusi. Courtesy of the Collection Museum of Modern Art.

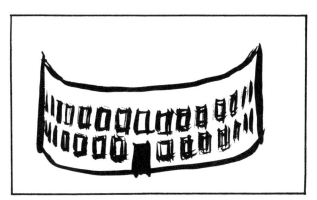

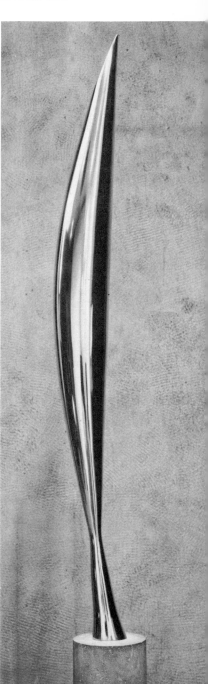

A few years ago, the newspapers featured what were called Droodles. These were physiognomic in nature, humorously conceived and popular for reasons of human imagination and participation. Two droodles, invented by the author, are shown in Figure 66. Captions could be as follows: Washington monument as seen by an architect wearing bifocal glasses (top); and apartment house built from set of curled blueprints (bottom). Most persons have seen faces in houses, any nature of things in clouds, rock formations and the like. The brain is never passive in what it sees. It keeps trying to imagine things, and the plastic arts may exploit all this to create new and dynamic forms.

In the fine arts, and in three dimensions, modern sculpture has created many effects of grace, character and power through physiognomic devices. Constantin Brancusi's "Bird in Space" is world famous. (See Figure 67.)

Henry Moore is recognized as one of the leading modern sculptors and has used physiognomic devices to aid his creative talents. (See Figure 68.)

Architecture today has begun to grasp the possibilities involved. Plates VI, VII and VIII show photographic examples of recent and outstanding work. The trend is away from the stolid and static to the curvilinear and flowing. Indeed, the architectural magazines, in America and throughout the world, are filled with examples that express a new spirit. A new and dynamic feeling for form—and color—is emerging. And the artist who will give thought to perception, to Gestalt factors, will profit tremendously.

In Plate IX, the author, with considerable assistance, has tried his hand at physiognomic expression. At the beginning of this chapter, mention was made of the immediacy of color in the perception of form. And Katz was quoted regarding the importance of color in the creation of form.

Inasmuch as *both color and form* may be coordinated to convey different visual and emotional impressions, there is a wonderful and engaging opportunity for the plastic arts to give original, inventive, and imaginative flight to an art of tomorrow.

Plate IX shows four forms in which shape and color are united to express that which is HOME-LIKE, SPIRITUAL, BLITHE and PRACTICAL. Although all persons by no means think and feel alike, none the less in physiognomic perception there seem to be qualities of reaction which are more or less universal. Art has this "psychology" to build upon and exploit. With modern building materials (stone, laminated wood, concrete) virtually anything may be achieved. The limitations of the post and lintel, the arch, the beam and girder, need no longer prove handicaps. If there is a new freedom as to structure, then there can be new freedom of design and conception.

The Gestalt psychologist may well deserve a physiognomically ordered monument in the future to acknowledge and pay tribute to his contributions.

Figure 68. "Reclining Figure," by Henry Moore. Courtesy of the Collection Museum of Modern Art.

4.

Good Organization and Control

Ruskin said that he did not consider architecture in any way perfect without color. By this, of course, he meant chromatic color. He contrasted architecture with sculpture, stating, "I would only note one point, that sculpture is the representation of an idea, while architecture is itself a real thing. The idea may, I think, be left colorless and colored by the beholder's mind; but a reality ought to have reality in all its attributes: its color should be as fixed as its form."

Virtually all architecture up to the time of the Renaissance was colored, either integrally (natural materials or ceramics) or applied. The temple at Karnak was brilliant with hue, and there are still vestiges of red on the face of the Sphinx. Ceramic art flourished throughout Mesopotamia. Oriental architecture has always been and still is colored. Classical Greek architecture did not feature raw marble, as many suppose. Most materials and surfaces were coated, an ivory wax being used to cover white. The Greek palette made free use of red, blue, gold, black. Rome was more conservative on exteriors; yet color was used lavishly, as at Pompeii. The Byzantine style was gaudy with colorful mosaics and marbles.

As to Gothic architecture, it was by no means as austere as one would assume in looking at surviving edifices today. Gothic buildings and monuments were freely colored inside and out; the facade of Notre Dame still bears traces of color. According to James Ward, "This coloring occurred principally on the moldings, columns, sculptured ornament and figure work. . . . There were bright reds, crude greens, orange, yellow ochre, blacks and pure whites."

PLATE X. *These buildings of antiquity were all adorned with color. Upper left is the Egyptian temple at Karnak. Upper right is the Tower of Babel, a ziggurat in Asia Minor. Lower left is the Greek Parthenon. Lower right is Notre Dame in Paris. (See page 75.)*

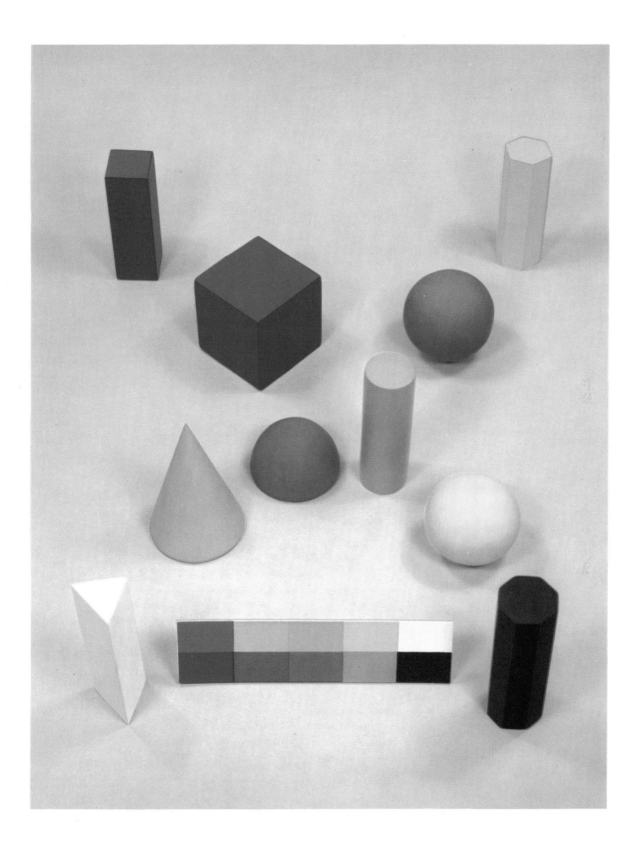

PLATE XI. A basic palette of colors having good tradition in architecture. These are the hues that seem to have universal qualities and to be repeated again and again— to great human pleasure. Most are related to primary elements in human perception. (See page 78.)

What happened? It is probable that the austerity of the Reformation drove the colorist away. In fact, it was the spirit of Luther, Wesley, Calvin, Knox and others which undoubtedly banished color from the temple and at the same time gave Western man an ascetic prejudice which only now is he finding himself able to overthrow without pangs of conscience. In 1652, one Elias Ashmole wrote of certain colorful decorations on the venerable walls of Westminster Abbey—"a faire large red rose," "a bright yellow glory." A person won't find them today. As Ashmole sadly related three hundred years ago, "Notwithstanding it has pleased some, to wash the *Originall* over with a *Plasterer's* whited *Brush*."

Renaissance architecture was a bewildering mixture. Its materials ranged in color from natural stone and brick, to the most exaggerated combinations of hued marble and granite, decorated by mosaic, fresco and encaustic painting, and just about every trick of the decorative trade.

In brief, the ancients built great masses of solid masonry, which they generously colored. The Greeks introduced geometry and proportion, and also delighted in color, but as if design was a property of material. The Romans engineered form in terms of solid weight and structure. The Gothic artists, with a knowledge of stresses and strains, "floating" ribs, slender columns, and flying buttresses, created effects which had the most intriguing of physiognomic qualities in the whole history of western architecture.

Then, in modern times, the steel girder and beam gave man a new freedom of space. Modern architecture became space architecture, with design, ornament, decoration stripped away. Form may follow function, but if it does so, there is sadness rather than joy in its heart. For functional architecture is essentially virile and naked. It is what it says and reveals, and there is little pride, vanity or mystery about it. And because there have been few men without pride, vanity, or mystery, so-called functional architecture has had the dull quality of a physiologist's chart. It has been architecture without a psyche.

Man needs an idealized portrait of himself, not an X-ray. Fortunately in architecture, a new movement is looming. There will be attention to man's desire and need to participate in what he sees, to add beauty from within himself. There will be movement, rhythm, ornamentation. The use of materials which shape and flow and are self supporting is coming fast (in poured concrete, laminated wood, forms and panels). There will be new materials, textures, and honest-to goodness acceptance of color as a natural phenomenon rather than a self-conscious convention.

A separate page of illustrations (Plate X) shows examples of architecture which were originally colored. (Plates VI, VII, and VIII have exhibited a few newer forms having a Gestalt quality.)

This chapter will discuss some practical architectural and design ideas which are more or less traditional in origin. Chapter 7 will venture into stranger and more original domains.

Color has definite visual order. This was discussed in Chapter 2 and diagrammed in Figure 40. When this natural and wholly psychological order is reduced to simple elements, architecture and design may work with "palettes" which are perceptually beautiful and which are endowed with sound Gestalt factors.

Many times the need of color is to have frank and direct appeal. It is debatable if color, particularly on the outside of buildings, should be subtle or primary. Much would depend, of course, on the purpose of the building and the design factors that have entered into it. Yet if color is to serve a social purpose—that is, appeal to the public at large—then too much that is personal, vague or ephemeral may miss its point. Creative effort should achieve beauty that may be universally recognized, and this in itself requires talent and skill.

See Figure 69. This charts color preferences as studied by many psychologists, and the facts relate to all persons, regardless of age or nationality. In the full spectrum, peaks are reached at blue, red and green, in this order.

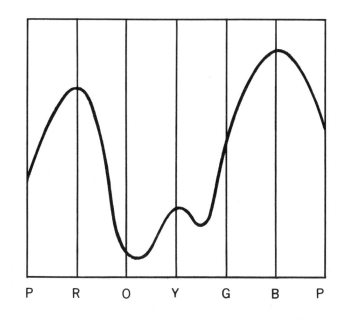

Figure 69. Color preference ratings. The peaks are at blue, red and green.

P   R   O   Y   G   B   P

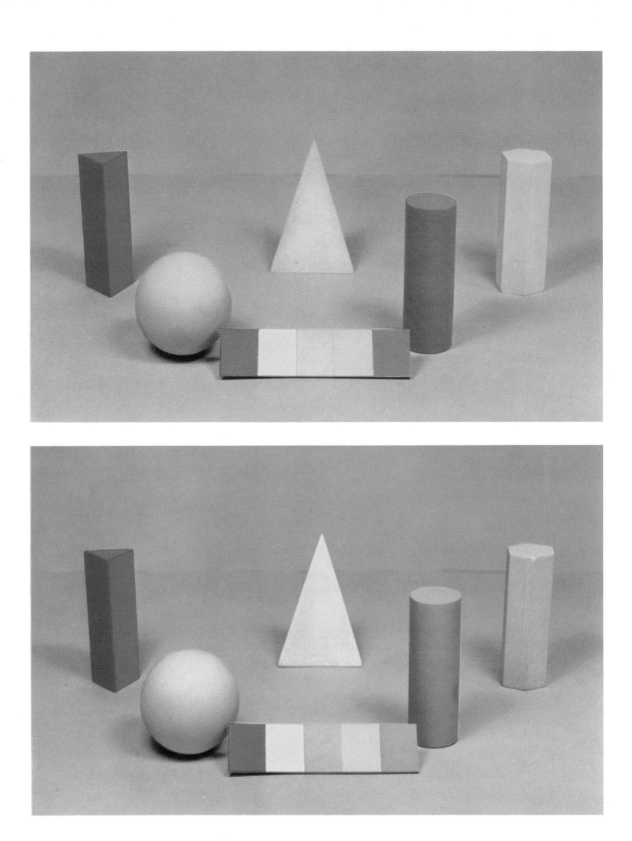

PLATE XII. *The upper illustration shows a well-balanced, warm palette in which five hues (red, yellow, green, blue, purple) are all shifted toward the orange region of the spectrum. The lower illustration shows a similar cool palette in which the five colors are shifted toward the blue region of the spectrum. Note harmonious relationships in both instances. (See page 79.)*

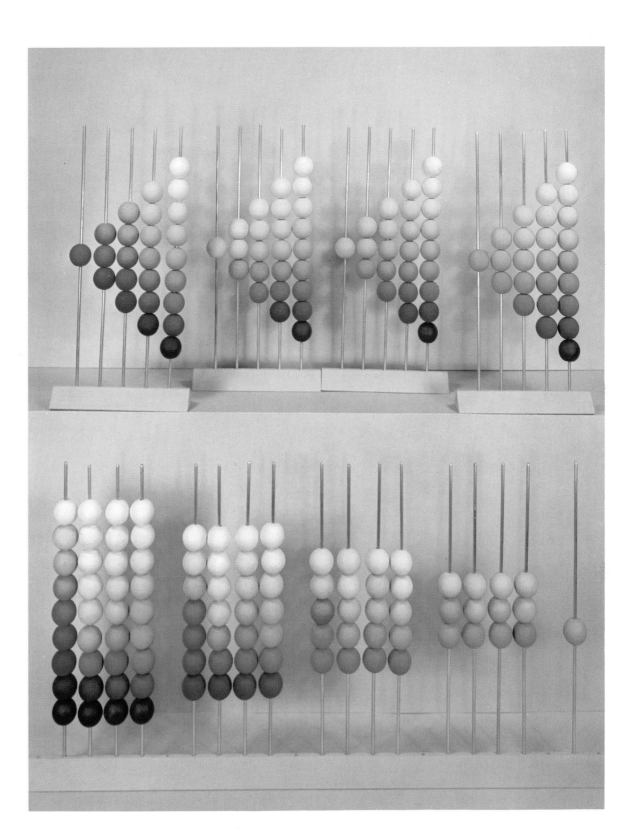

PLATE XIII. The Color Triangle in plastic form, as described in the text. Across the top are well-related tints, shades and tones of 4 pure hues. At the bottom the layers or envelopes have been "peeled" away to show concordant relationships. Note diminishing series toward gray, to agree with "laws" of perception. (See page 81.)

The least preferred hues are purple, yellow and orange. It should be recognized that man has strong emotional feelings about color and will react agreeably or disagreeably to what he sees. In commercial enterprises, such as stores, off-beat colors, such as purples, and olives, have been known to repel trade. Why not? If a store displays, on its walls, colors which people do not like, the merchandise will not sell. And if the general atmosphere of the store is not favored, the customer may turn on his or her heel.

The point is often missed that color for the sake of color is not enough. Nor is individual taste ever assured of mass acceptance. To repeat, people respond emotionally toward color. They are patriotic—almost religious—about their predilections. Decorate or adorn a beautiful form in a disliked hue, and it will be rejected.

Although blue, red and green are the most liked of all hues, yellow may be admitted to the list. It has a bright luminous charm and seems to be well accepted in architectural work. The same, however, cannot be said of orange and purple.

Plate XI shows the elementary palette described above. It comprises a bright red and a garnet red, a turquoise blue and a royal blue, a cool green and a deep green, a clear yellow and a gold, white and black.

I by no means argue that such a color selection is better than any other. It definitely is not, and other palettes are to follow. But if an architect or designer were to "research" what people like in color, the standards of Plate XI would undoubtedly win out over most others. If mass appeal is to be assured, if the public at large is to respond favorably, an artist could hardly do better than to cater to its psychology. Maybe this would limit such a color selection to world fairs, places of amusement, commercial edifices. However, do not hold the illusion that primary colors are in any way vulgar or commonplace. They have the same Gestalt as simple forms. Fashion is what is ephemeral. The artist is great who will glorify the simple element (like a symphony composed from a folk tune), and give it uncommon beauty. He will be quite certain of universal praise.

Primary colors elicit a direct, impulsive reaction. For this reason, they are best suited to applications where spontaneous appeal is wanted—a building exterior, lobby, etc. In applications involving more deliberate inspection, for interiors occupied for long periods of time, primary colors are likely to prove somewhat monotonous.

There are many ways of organizing the spectrum to agree with good psychological and visual order. Chapter 2 spoke of qualities of warmth and coolness in color, or of what the Gestalt psychologist terms hardness and softness. Not only are certain hues warm (red, orange, yellow) and cool (green, blue, violet), but every simple color has its warm or cool variation. Warmth is in the direction of orange; coolness is in the direction of blue.

Refer to Figure 70 and the upper illustration of Plate XII. Figure 70 plots a color circle having five hues (similar to Munsell): red, yellow, green, blue, violet (or purple). To give it warmth, the red is moved toward vermilion, the yellow made more of a chrome, the green moved toward chartreuse, the blue kept toward ultramarine, and the violet shifted toward magenta. In the top demonstration of Plate XII the general effect is on the warm side, with all colors bearing consistent and harmonious relationship to each other. The palette is still a red, yellow, green, blue one (with violet added). It may no longer be elemental, but it still plays on visual chords in which most people delight.

In Figure 71 and the lower illustration of Plate XII, a cool palette is developed. Here all colors are moved toward blue. The red is made purplish, the yellow given a lemon tinge, the green shifted toward blue, the blue kept true in character, and the violet inclined toward so-called indigo. Again the arrangement is concordant—and the primary colors (plus violet) effectively ennobled.

Color harmony like this is not academic, nor is it worked out in accordance with technically systematized color arrangements. Rather, it respects psychological and Gestalt principles. This approach has always been preferred by me, for I have resisted color systems as being too dogmatic and too far removed from the facts of human perception.

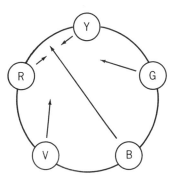

Figure 70. Development
of a warm palette.

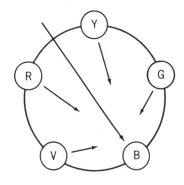

Figure 71. Development
of a cool palette.

PLATE XIV. The upper illustration shows seven pairs of traditional or conservative colors, all having a refined quality and all suggesting a certain refined elegance. The lower illustration shows seven pairs of so-called modern or contemporary colors. Here the hues are cleaner and sharper. There is coordination and harmony in both groups. (See page 84.)

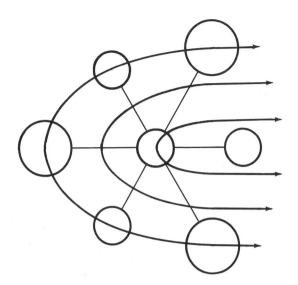

Figure 72. Layers or en-velopes of the Color Tri-angle.

However, if order in color is to be followed, the best to be found would be that indicated in the Color Triangle of Figure 40 and discussed in Chapter 2. (See also Figure 43 which points out the beauty of scales that run in straight lines on the Triangle.)

Now by "peeling" layers or envelopes from the Color Triangle, the artist will have a series of scales or palettes in ideal harmony. See Figure 72 and Plate XIII. Here the Triangle has been given nine steps on the vertical gray axis and plotted in diminishing steps toward a full hue. I have used a warm red, a yellow, a warm green and a turquoise, but colors of any other hue could be similarly arranged.

Across the top of Plate XIII are the complete sections in the four hues, painted on wooden beads and photographed in color. (Note that color scales or sequences run neatly in any horizontal, vertical or diagonal direction.)

However, in the bottom illustration of Plate XIII, the layers have been peeled away, as indicated in Figure 72, and stacked in vertical rows. Note the following:

The outer layer comprises the four full hues scaled toward white and toward black. None of these colors contains gray. All look near to the eye for this reason. Being near in quality, good discrimination is possible, and the scales have nine steps (including black and white).

In the second series toward the right is the second layer or envelope. These colors have a slightly grayish quality and have end points in a light and a deep gray. The number of beads has diminished to seven in each row.

In the third series, the scales are even grayer, and have diminished to five.

In the fourth series, approaching a middle gray, the scales have diminished to three.

PLATE XV. *Ideal tones, as described in the text. Colors of any hue may be adjusted in brightness between black and white, and in chroma between purity and gray, and will provide effective backgrounds. Across the top is an ideal tone of blue-green which is a flattering complement to the pinkish tint of human complexion. (See page 86.)*

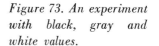

Figure 73. An experiment with black, gray and white values.

It is a fact of perception that colors become grayer as they recede into distance, and that because sharp acuity is lost, the eye is less able to distinguish brightness differences. That is, more color variations can be seen up close than far away. Indeed, if the reader will study perceptible differences in the color scales of Plate XIII, he will note that they are relatively the same throughout. The "clean" scales, nine in number, appear as neatly removed from each other in visual difference as the grayish scales which have seven, five or only three steps.

Color palettes of this sort are beautifully adapted to the needs of architecture and industrial design. They imply aerial perspective quite effectively, moving from near to far and diminishing in scale as they do so.

Forms are to be given dramatic and pleasing relationship through their use. Near forms may be given the full scale of the outer layer. Forms which fall back—or which rise high—may be modified. Everything will look right for the good reason that laws of perception will be respected.

Figure 73, in black and white, expresses all this in an elementary way. A form having four stages is progressively foreshortened from bottom to top in logarithmic steps. The lower stage is given seven gray steps from black to white. The middle five of these gray steps are used in the second stage, the middle three in the fourth, and the remaining (middle) gray at the top. Although the values are repeated, each stage is well unified and each falls back (or rises) in convincing fashion.

If you wish to give order to color, let the facts of human vision serve as a guide.

As has been said, primary colors are likely to have a direct, frank appeal. They are probably best where masses of people are to be pleased emotionally. Yet there are times where more subtlety and personality may have the right of expression.

Although I usually avoid strict rules or any conventions which are limiting or arbitrary in scope, I do take the liberty of talking about the elements of perception, and feel rather sure that the artist will be able to follow me (since he has the same human experience himself). I further assume that to "brush up" on his knowledge of scientific and Gestalt factors in vision will help to broaden the artist's viewpoint and add greater skill to his native talents. Thus I make the plea that this chapter—and the whole book, in fact—be liberally considered as a sincere effort on my part, not to confine the world of color, but to break open new frontiers. I have endeavored to express principles not doctrines, and to demonstrate what I mean in general rather than specific terms. I leave final and advanced expression to the artist.

Refer to Plate XIV. Let the elementary palette of Plate XI be set aside for a different concept of color; this one embodies a more esthetic and refined concept. In general, most human beings may be classified as either introverted or extroverted, to use Carl Jung's terms. Some are contemplative (the introverts), rational, deliberate and "inwardly oriented." They tend to be influenced, if at all, by their own judgment. On the other hand, some are impulsive (the extroverts), "outwardly oriented," and tend to be influenced by the circumstances of the world about them. They are the impressionable ones.

In the Rorschach ink blot test, the introverts are likely to hide their feelings, while the extroverts usually respond more freely. The subjective types tend to analyze things—and color—in personal terms, while the objective types are given to less personal reflection. It has also been noted by psychologists that introverts are chiefly affected by form, and extroverts by color. (See Figure 74.)

In any event, there are different types when it comes to color preference. The introverts are likely to delight in refined hues, and in traditional interior decoration and architectural styles. The extroverts, being more liberal in view, are likely to choose brighter hues and a contemporary look in interior decoration and architecture. Thus no one taste is better than another; much depends on individual personality.

Plate XIV expresses the color preferences of the two temperaments—for

Figure 74. The contemplative and the garrulous types, from an old engraving.

interior as well as exterior use. The architect or designer may definitely prefer one group of colors to the other, and if he does, he may thereby identify himself as an introvert or extrovert.

In the upper part of Plate XIV are the conservative or traditional colors. These all have a subtle quality. Arranged in pairs, they include: two shades of rose; two shades of gold; a pale grayish blue and a slate blue; a sage green and an olive green; a mauve and a purple; a beige and a brown; and a putty color and a taupe. Persons who are introspective in nature may well prefer them by and large. They have good tradition and look harmonious with traditional styles of decoration and architecture.

In the lower part of Plate XIV are the more directly appealing, contemporary colors. In pairs, they include: a pink and coral; a yellow and black; an aqua and turquoise; a cool light green and a forest green; a clear blue on the light and dark side; a red and maroon; and a gray and charcoal. Once again, the less restrained person may embrace the lot as expressing his more dynamic feelings. They have a modern appearance and seem to lend themselves appropriately to modern decoration and architecture.

The two palettes of Plate XIV are "livable" colors in the sense that they depart from the primary and, at the same time, hold psychological significance. They will stand viewing over long periods of time without becoming unduly monotonous. They are offered to the artist, not as prescriptions, but as menus which he may use to assure a varied fare of color as circumstances may suggest.

Finally, a few words about what may be called ideal tones for color. It has been mentioned that the tone—not gray, white or black—is the most neutral of all color forms. The reason is that the tone combines all primary elements —pure color, white and black. Technically, perhaps, a purplish tone would be the best foil or background for the display of other colors, inasmuch as it is passive and retiring and blends the two ends of the spectrum, warm red and cool blue. Purple, however, is not a well-liked color, so a bluish tone might be more desirable.

Refer to Plate XV and Figure 75. In developing an ideal tone of any hue, the process is simply one (a) of getting a value midway between white and black, and (b) a chroma midway between full purity and neutral gray. Depending on lighting conditions, the middle value will probably be on the light side and have a reflectance of about 25 or 30 per cent. If the tone is to be used for an interior, and if light will be on the dim side (a living room, for example), an even lighter value may be necessary to gain the balanced effect wanted. The best way to bring the ideal tone to perfection is to experiment with it under the illumination in which it is to be seen and applied.

At the top of Plate XV an ideal tone of blue-green (turquoise) is shown.

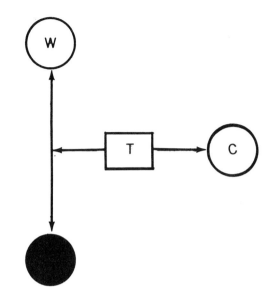

Figure 75. The develop-
ment of ideal color tones.

It has been modified, as described, to give approximately equal visibility for white, for black, for neutral gray and for pure blue-green itself—all at the same time. Blue-green is the direct complement or opposite of average flesh and has a warm pinkish afterimage. It is probably the most flattering of all colors in the spectrum for this reason. It has almost countless uses.

Otherwise in Plate XV, ideal tones are shown for red (rose), yellow (gold), blue, green and purple. Each has its particular beauty, is most "livable" and has a refinement which represents one of the most subtle expressions of color design.

The old assumption that gray is the most neutral of color forms is easily upset. The Gestalt psychologist has noted that colors "segregate" oddly with gray. The reason is that the quality of hue is totally lacking in gray and therefore tends to produce conflict. But combine white, black, and *hue* in one tone, and all primary color forms will be accounted for.

An ideal tone, of course, must comprise a hue of some sort. Will this hue conflict with other hues? It may, but the chances are unlikely for the good reason that the ideal tone is always soft, modified and therefore retiring. A blue-green tone, as a case in point, will neatly display almost any other color, red, yellow, green, blue—even pure turquoise itself. The only thing that may be lost is the blue-green tone itself. But this would happen with any matching background color.

5.

The Human Nature of Illumination

This chapter will present new principles of color based on the perception of illumination and the phenomena of color constancy. The color palettes described in previous chapters and illustrated in Plates XI to XV may have a familiar look, for they represent refinements of traditions which have been a part of art and architecture in the past. Here we will deal with effects which are less familiar and draw upon more advanced concepts in the art of color.

A quick review seems in order. First of all, I make no attempt to discuss formal theories of color harmony, for most of them are academic. Color should be given free expression. If any qualifications or advice are necessary, they concern simple visual laws and the facts of psychological reaction.

It will be pertinent to summarize some of the points of Chapter 3.

—The Color Triangle (Figure 40) plots the natural order of color in human perception.

—Colors have different modes of appearance: film, volume, surface, etc.

—It is fairly easy to account for the visibility of color, its attentive powers, and the like.

—Light and warm colors appear nearer and larger than grayish and cool colors.

—Dark colors seem heavier than light colors.

On perspective and space relations—of considerable significance to the

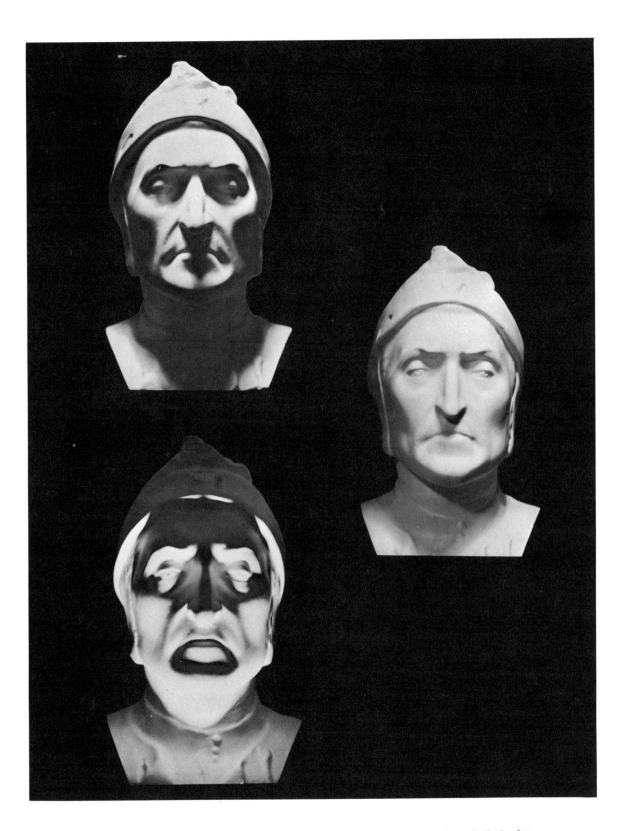

PLATE XVI. Dante as he might appear in heaven, on earth, and in hell. Lighting can be effectively and dramatically used to convey markedly different emotional impressions. Perception, for example, generally expects illumination to come from above. Where this situation is reversed, very weird and unreal visual experiences can be gained. (See page 91.)

PLATE XVII. *Four views which show various daylight conditions: full sunlight, an overcast sky, dusk or darkness, mist. These natural effects can be arbitrarily controlled to serve high purposes in plastic design. (See page 97.)*

plastic arts—here are some of the clues by which the eye orients itself to the world and separates the near from the far.

—Brightness and lightness dominate darkness.

—Pure color appears more forward than grayed color.

—Warm color advances, while cool color retires.

—Detail, texture, roundness, a sense of structure and solidity will distinguish near things, while far things appear plainer, flatter and more filmy.

—Highlights and cast shadows contribute to plastic form.

—Perspective guides vision. An object, which is in front of another object and partially covers it, is perceived as nearer.

—The apparent size of recognizable objects effectively establishes positions in space.

However, illumination comes first and reveals the world to man.

There are many simple and observable facts about illumination which seem to go unnoticed by architects and designers. What is significant from the standpoint of art is that if nature changes and modifies forms with light and atmosphere, man holds the power of *implying* these same things in his creative expression and hence putting natural phenomena to singular and dramatic use.

Except for a few subjective experiences (afterimages), the world is revealed to the eye through light. Illumination creates and destroys space, and it changes the aspects of things in endless ways. Lighting can be used to express different emotional effects, as illustrated in Plate XVI. The three photographs show a bust of Dante lighted from above, below, and one side.

Space itself is perceived when objects are illuminated. The earth seems wider, broader and more infinite where there is bright light. In darkness, the world crowds in. In total darkness, a person has the sense of a dark (not black) conical "emptiness" which, while it extends into distance, does not extend very far.

Forms are round and three-dimensional under bright sunlight which is directional, but flatten out under dim light or under the influence of atmosphere, which are more diffuse. See Figure 76.

In a similar way, plain surfaces when seen at a distance, particularly under dim light, may confuse judgments of distance and space. The effect may be wanted or unwanted. When a person enters a planetarium, he may be quite conscious that a structural dome is overhead. In total darkness, this overhead may seem to disappear, but space will still be confused. Yet when stars and planets are projected, a perfect illusion of infinite space is achieved.

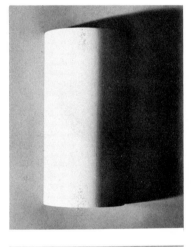

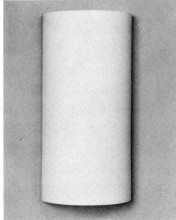

Figure 76. The appearance of forms under directional and diffuse light.

C

A

B

See Figure 77. A plain area under dim light may appear vaguely flat or uncertain (A). Where details are seen within it, the surface or area will be definitely localized (B). However, if the area is dotted with point light sources—and the surrounding space left dark and plain—vast space may be successfully implied (C). Here three different effects—all useful in architecture—may be established with more or less the same structural elements.

To some extent, man is able to judge distance and space in the mechanical workings of depth perception. The eye muscles used in convergence and accommodation tell him whether things are near or far. He may also refer to orientation points in his field of vision.

In near-darkness, however, he isn't too expert. If a man carrying a lantern on a very dark night is moving away from an observer, his position will be accurately judged for only a short distance—possibly a few hundred yards. If darkness surrounds the lantern, and if the man continues to move, it would be difficult to judge if he were one mile, or a thousand miles away. On the horizon, indeed, his lantern might be confused with a rising star or planet. Hence illusions of great space are not difficult if there is careful control of brightness and illumination.

It is a strange truth that man looks upon darkness as something quite

Figure 77. Plain surfaces under dim light (A) may appear vague and indefinite. Where detail is seen (B), the surface will appear structured and localized. Where point light sources are introduced (C), infinite space may be well implied.

tangible and powerful. At dusk, one does not consider approaching night as a *retreat* of light. On the contrary, night "falls"; it rolls in like a gigantic tide and seems to push the last rays of the sun over the horizon. At the same time, the stars *come out*—they were gone or were far away during the day.

In the visual perception of lightness and darkness, color and space, the next chapter will discuss one of the most curious and remarkable of all visual and perceptional phenomena—color constancy. David Katz writes, "The way in which we see the color of a surface is in large measure independent of the intensity and wave-length of the light it reflects, and at the same time definitely dependent upon the nature and intensity of the illumination in which it appears."

To explain this rather enigmatic statement, note that Katz distinguishes between *light* and *illumination*. This is the key. Assume that a white card taken into the open on a clear day reflects 1,000 units (footlamberts) of *light*. If clouds suddenly appeared and the sky grew dim, the card might now reflect 500 units. Then if it began to rain and the card were taken indoors, it might reflect only 1 unit. Yet in all cases the card would still appear white, thus bearing out, as Katz says, that "the color of a surface is in large measure independent of the intensity . . . of the *light* it reflects."

However, if the card were isolated from its environment and viewed through a hole in a black screen, its constancy (whiteness) might be lost or confused. The eye, to hold constancy of color, needs to see the whole environment. The phenomenon, again to quote Katz, is "definitely dependent upon the nature and intensity of the *illumination* in which it [the color] appears."

In other words, the eye judges color largely in terms of the general illumination in which it is seen. It does not respond in terms of light energy alone, like a photoelectric cell. The whole process of constancy involves visual and mental interpretation.

This sense of illumination—which at the same time involves a sense of space—holds significance in two ways. First, an understanding of it will help to explain many natural phenomena and sharpen the artist's powers of observation. Second, it may be turned to new expressions in architecture and design. Nature's own processes may be repeated under controlled conditions and applied in many original and creative ways. Best of all, the very *psychology* of illumination and color—which is personal to the experience, sensation and perception of all persons—may be turned to new art forms. The designer will not be following cold and external rules, but will be dealing with the fascinating stuff of his own consciousness.

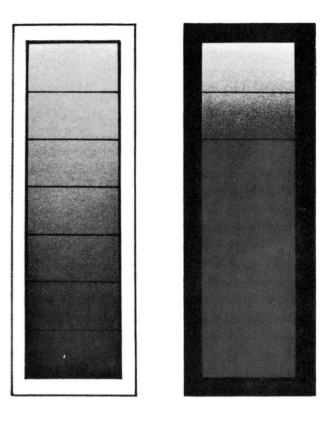

Figure 78. A gray scale as seen under normal light (left) and dim light (right).

As the next chapter will make clear, because of color constancy the eye holds remarkable consistent impressions of color and brightness under decidedly different conditions of light energy. For the present, however, extreme effects will be discussed which lie beyond the normal thresholds of color constancy.

Study Figure 78. When a gray scale is seen in normal light, all its steps are quite perceptible. As illumination grows dim, however, the top end (white) maintains a fair degree of lightness, but the lower values melt together and lose distinction. Now one sees really two values, a confined light area and a broad dark area. The dark area, incidentally, is a deep gray rather than black, for black needs bright light to be seen as such.

In dark-adaptation, the human eye loses a sense of values. If the illumination is feeble, the sensation of color will no longer be experienced. In technical terms, any color or color value reflecting less than 20 per cent of light will appear black (deep gray). Clear perception of surface colors will be next to impossible. Night is essentially dark in major area, offset by touches of light. Colors disappear and forms appear flat and in silhouette. They will further look filmy and will lose surface texture.

One important lesson is to be learned here. Color schemes worked out in normal light may collapse in dim light. Medium and deep colors (any areas reflecting less than 20 per cent) will have little or no meaning. If a person has a liking for black, for maroon, forest green, navy blue, brown, and any such dark shades, he will need good light for them to be perceived. If the area being designed is to be seen under dim lighting conditions, it is not only best but sensible to work with medium tones, since they are the only ones that will have any visual significance. In fact, they will look no different than darker colors.

When the eye is light-adapted, it sees colors and values in a normal way. The dark-adapted eye is not so discriminating. Whereas yellow is the color of highest visibility in bright light, the shift is toward green in dim light. (See Figure 79.) Normal colors in highlight move up the color circle toward the hue of next higher value. In shadow they will move down toward the color

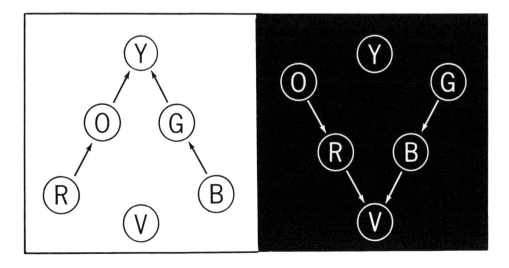

Figure 79. Colors tend to swing toward yellow in highlight and toward violet in shadow.

next lower value. Red, for example, will be orange in highlight and purplish in shadow. Green will become yellower in highlight and bluer in shadow. Blue will become greener in highlight and more violet in shadow. But if illumination really darkens, all sense of color will be lost—and colors of long wave length (reds) will fade out sooner than colors of short wave length (blues).

Now refer to Figure 80, and compare it with Figure 78. As forms fall back into distance and are influenced by atmosphere, they tend to approach a medium light gray. This is true of values which scale from white to black. Colors also shift toward muted tones of gray.

This is aerial perspective, noted by many great painters such as da Vinci and made a part of landscape art for a number of centuries. The Old Masters, in fact, often used one palette for the foreground, one for the middle ground, and one for the distinct background.

What is significant to modern concepts of plastic forms is well expressed by Arnheim. "Aerial perspective is effective, however, not because it is natural, but because it produces a perceptual gradient. It can be used at small distances, where the influence of the air is negligible."

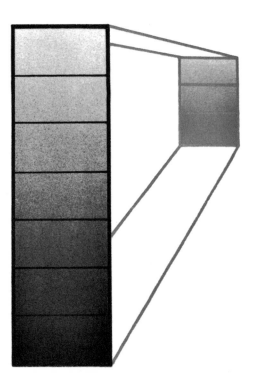

Figure 80. Colors and forms tend to approach a medium light gray in distance.

Plate XVII shows four black and white photographs of Fifth Avenue taken from my office window in New York. One is under full sunlight (A), one under an overcast sky (B), one at dusk (C), and one in mist (D). Each has its charm, but each is the result of nature's versatility.

In sunlight, there is a full revelation of light and dark, shadows and highlights. The overcast sky flattens the buildings and probably detracts from the play of light and shade that the architects originally planned. In dim light (twilight), the structures become flat, and one sees luminous spots shining from the windows. In mist (as in Figure 80), the whole scene softens down to a pale gray having minimum contrast.

Assume now that such effects were deliberately planned, and suppose that the architect or designer devised exterior color schemes to glorify them. In other words, he puts aerial perspective into the materials of his building and exhibits them accordingly—under normal light, and in emulation of nature herself.

In Figure 81, aerial perspective has been arbitrarily applied to a vertical structure having three stages. The bottom stage is dark, the center stage medium, and the upper stage pale. Note how the forms recede harmoniously as they extend upward. This would be a pleasing sight because it would agree with the common experience of perception. Such an edifice (in gray or any other color) would, if seen from street level, seem altogether natural. The upper stages would float skyward, seem lighter in weight and (if details were also modified) would carry out, under an artist's direction, what nature herself does.

In Plate XVIII, three color schemes have similarly been designed. The effects you see were put into the forms themselves, and they were all photographed under the same lighting conditions.

In the top photograph, the forms were plainly painted in yellow, green and blue. Lighting from the sides has given them a slight indication of shape.

In the middle photograph, the forms were carefully but deliberately shaded to imply dim illumination. Note that the highlight colors are as pure as in the top photograph. Here there is a rich, deep beauty and a wholly different mood.

In the bottom photograph, the forms were colored to appear as if in mist. There is still a different mood, possibly the most refined and agreeable of all.

Architecture has such phenomena at its command—to use creatively in original ways. Couple a knowledge of illumination with that of color constancy and new visions will take shape—as I hope to demonstrate in the next two chapters.

PLATE XVIII. Arbitrary control of illumination effects in plastic forms. In the upper illustration, the colors are solid. In the center, the forms have been shaded to imply slightly suppressed illumination. In the lower, the forms were toned toward gray to imply distance or atmosphere. Here natural phenomena are put under control of the artist.

6.

The Magic of Color Constancy

Color constancy is one of the most fascinating of all visual phenomena. It represents a common experience that may go unnoticed during most of a person's lifetime. Its study in human perception has waited for modern times and the inquiries of the psychologist. Perhaps the best book on the subject, though a bit out of date, is *The World of Color* by David Katz.

The many subtleties of color constancy have led to new expressions for color—which will be illustrated in this and the following chapter. This subject is also discussed in my book, *Creative Color*.

Color constancy relates to the startling and fully observable fact that the colors of the world maintain a normal and uniform appearance under marked changes in light intensity. What exists in the world of light energy is amazingly independent of what takes place in human perception. Indeed, the psychology of vision is a lot nearer to the interests of the artist than is the science of physics.

Perform the simple experiment shown in Figure 82 which is derived from Ewald Hering. Place a white card (B) on a window sill. Standing inside a room, and facing the light, hold a second white card (A), which has a hole in it, and look through this hole at card B. If cards A and B are held on the same horizontal plane, both whites will have the same brightness.

Now if card A is tilted toward the light, it will reflect more daylight and become brighter. At once card B will look deeper and grayer. Conversely, if card A is tilted back to reflect less light, card B will appear to increase in brightness. What is notable here is that card A keeps a white appearance even though it reflects different intensities of light as it is tilted toward and away from the window. However, card B, which remains stationary and which always reflects the same volume of light, appears to shift in brightness from light to dark. The card that changes (A) will tend to look the same, and the card that does not change (B) will take on different shades.

If the sensations of color (and brightness) were strictly dependent on reactions to stimuli, the world might present a weird aspect. A white surface would turn gray if a cloud passed over the sun; pastel tints in a garden would become tones or shades. However, color constancy is ever on the job telling you that white is white (or red is red, etc.) whether you see it at dawn, midday or dark. Colors may not be *exactly* the same, but they will remain surprisingly uniform.

In the previous chapter, reference was made to color appearances (and value changes) under bright and dim illumination. This data still holds true. In dealing with color constancy, *normal* ranges of light intensity are concerned, not extreme ones. This on an average would involve intensities of light anywhere from about 5 to 5,000 footcandles.

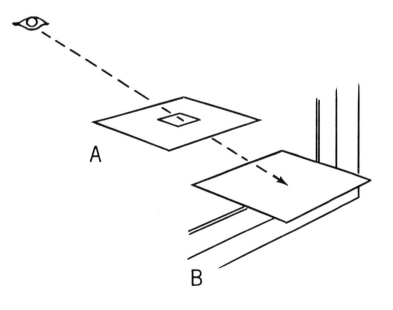

Figure 82. Hering's experiment.

Figure 83. White, gray and black forms — normally exposed (upper), underexposed (center), and overexposed (bottom).

Figure 84. The phenomenon of color constancy.

The eye has upper and lower thresholds. In the full brilliance of sunlight there may be an overabundance of energy—too much light for the eye to handle with comfort. A person may therefore shade his eyes, squint, or wear sunglasses to reduce the illumination and pull it down to a more reasonable level. Similarly in darkness, the eye may be strained to see, and artificial sources will be called upon for help.

Yet within these extremes—blazing sunlight and complete darkness—normal illumination is found and color constancy is quite ideal.

Because of color constancy, there is no such thing (within reasonable limits) of underexposure or overexposure in human vision. On this point, the eye is quite unlike a camera and will, in fact, put a camera to shame.

Look at the three photographs in Figure 83. In the original setup there were three cards in white, gray and black. When the camera was properly adjusted, the three values were accurately reproduced, as shown in the top photograph. In the middle photograph, one sees the results of underexposure, and in the bottom, the results of overexposure. Nothing like this happens in visual experience, for color constancy would retain a sense of white, gray and black, regardless of light intensity (except in the case of extreme brilliance or extreme darkness).

The camera is particularly baffled when it attempts to deal with different lighting conditions at one and the same time. Thus when two white cards are set up, one near the light source and one away from it, and photographed, the near card appears white, but the far card appears gray (Figure 84). Yet in viewing this scene, both cards will persist in appearing white. This is color constancy. Unlike a camera, the eye cannot be made to see white in a gray surface that is showered with bright illumination. Nor can it be made to see gray in a white surface deprived of light.

Genuine color is that term applied by Katz to hues and values seen in normal light and when color constancy is ideal. More than this, normal light assures a sense of accuracy in color discrimination and the perception of surface structure, three-dimensional form, size, distance, space. Katz uses another term—pronouncedness. A white in bright light has a high degree of pronouncedness; in softer illumination it will have lower pronouncedness, but it will remain essentially white.

Color constancy has been discussed at some length, because understanding

Figure 85. Cameras and eyes do not record the same facts.

and control of this phenomenon have led to unusual color effects, as will be seen.

The experiment shown in Figure 85 is derived from Katz and explains the difference between brightness and color as seen by the human eye and as it might be measured with a photometer or camera. In the top photograph, two white rectangles are set up and separated by a partition. Both rectangles are recorded as white when uniform illumination is distributed over them.

Now if the light is directed from the side, the partition casts a shadow over the rectangle to the right, as shown in the middle photograph. The result, *in the photograph*, is now a white rectangle and a gray one. Yet in *actual vision*, both rectangles will remain white, the only difference being that the left one will have higher pronouncedness than the right.

Now study the bottom photograph in Figure 85. This will require some attention, for the photograph contradicts the facts of the original setup. The same lighting condition as the middle photograph was maintained. However, a *gray* rectangle was placed at the left, the brightness of which apparently matched the brightness of the *white* rectangle at the right which was in shadow. The bottom photograph shows two gray rectangles which are relatively the same. But what the eye saw was a gray rectangle at the left and a white rectangle (in shadow) at the right.

Color constancy requires a general view of an environment. If the experiments described above (Figure 85), are viewed through aperture screens (black cards with holes in them), constancy will be lost; the eye and brain will not be able to grasp the situation at large. Also, the more natural a scene, the easier color constancy operates. Vernon points out that it is best maintained where there are various colors, forms, and familiar objects in view. If surroundings are flat or homogeneous, the eye may be somewhat confused.

Try this simple experiment. Sit at a window during the day with a white aperture screen in your hand. At the far end of the room place a large white card or piece of cloth. You will be able to glance from one to the other and see them both as white (a feat beyond the capability of a camera). However, if you glance at the far white area through the hole in the aperture screen, its genuine color may be lost. It may, indeed, appear definitely dark gray or even black.

Do not assume that color constancy is to be attributed to intelligence, experience or reason. It is observable in animals. A hen, for example, can be trained to eat nothing but white grains of rice by gluing red grains down to a board. Within a short time the hen will solve the problem and fill her gizzard with white food. Now if red light is introduced, the white grains will, in fact, not be white but red—and virtually the same as the dyed red grain. None the less, the hen will continue as she did before.

It is in the realm of color that constancy phenomena are most unusual—and most useful for the purposes of art. For man sees the world as normal, not only as light intensity changes, but as the chromatic tint of light is also changed. If light is rather moderately tinted, adaptation to it will be unnoticed. Just as shifts in the *brightness* of daylight are taken by the eye in good visual stride, so the pink tint of twilight, the yellow of sunlight, the blue of the north sky seem to be more or less one and the same thing. In wearing a pair of tinted sunglasses, a gently chromatic world will promptly fade to normality.

A lot depends on the illumination quality of the general field of view. If you stand in a room at night illuminated by incandescent light, the window of a room across the way having fluorescent light will seem bluish. The room in which you stand will be the normal one. Reverse the condition, stand in the fluorescent room, and the window of the room illuminated with incandescent light will appear quite yellowish. (This shadow boxes set up in the lighting field to show the color quality of different light sources are misleading. What the eye sees in small area will always be judged and influenced by the color quality of the room in which a person stands.)

Color constancy under chromatic (tinted) light has amazingly wide limits. To quote Vernon, "Again, a white surface in a red light may up to a point appear less red than a red surface in white illumination, even when the former reflects more red light than the latter."

While constancy is less for colored light than it is for neutral "white" light, nevertheless, the eye shows much genius. Harry Nelson found that neutral (white, gray) surfaces retained their genuine appearance even when over 90 per cent of the incandescent light was chromatic. And colored surfaces maintained a remarkably higher degree of constancy. As Katz has put it, "The impression of an object's color is notably independent of the local stimulus situation."

These considerations lead to the Law of Field Size and the demonstrations presented with the next chapter. This principle is discussed in detail in *Creative Color*, mainly in relation to two-dimensional color effects. (Perceptionism is the term I use.) Here, however, color effects and expressions in *three dimensions* are featured, and this I believe to be quite new.

In the plastic arts, in architecture and industrial design, many of the phenomena of perception are to be given esthetic applications. If the human eye is able to see things, not merely in terms of the facts of stimulation, but in ways which are individual to man's psychological makeup, then it becomes possible to reverse the process, play with sensation itself and lead the eye to see imaginatively rather than literally. This approach is quite the opposite of that taken by artists of old who looked upon beauty as an intrinsic part of their creations. Today, in the wonders of perception, the artist may leave much unsaid, knowing that his viewer will respond and experience the pleasure of adding his own vision to that of the artist.

In the previous chapter on illumination (and in Plate XVIII), plastic forms were described in which appearances of dim light and mist were arbitrarily conceived. Impressions, or effects, of illumination were designed. Though based on natural phenomena, the eye, *upon seeing them under normal light,* used experience and perception to see them as if under modified light. The result was unique, to say the least.

Now, all visual sensations owe their existence to illumination. And illumination is perceived through the appearance of things seen in the field of view. General brightness implies bright light; general darkness implies dim light. This is perhaps academic. However, through new devices in art, illumination effects are to be *suggested* which do not run true to the facts of physical stimulation. The eye may be led to see more than actually meets it—and in the process art can find new roads of expression and put human perception through many exciting traces.

For example, if forms or patterns are slightly suppressed in color tone to imply dim light, pure touches, when added, can be made to appear lustrous, luminous or iridescent by comparison.

If the additive nature of light mixtures is studied and adapted to pigments and materials, forms can be made to appear as if modeled with chromatic light.

If a group of colors is organized and reproduced as if it is pervaded by colored light, it will hold this appearance when seen under normal light.

If colors seen through mist are modified by atmosphere, these modifications, carefully duplicated, will produce the same effect when a form or pattern is seen up close. (And the mist, incidentally, can be made to appear tinted in colors which nature has never troubled to employ.)

Perception, so long ignored, may be inspired to do more than record what is seen, but to get up on the stage set by the artist and take part in the drama of color.

7.

New Expressions for the Future

Plate XVIII and Chapter 5 on illumination have marked a beginning which points toward new color expressions for the future. However, a new viewpoint is necessary. The architect and designer must think less in terms of color as something existing in the world which the eye merely records in a matter-of-fact way, and more in terms of a dynamic role for perception. Sensations will be experienced and interpretations will be made which differ in a human way from the actual physical situations which happen to exist.

Let me begin with a demonstration and then discuss principles as I go along. Study Plate XIX. Here a simple architectural form has been colored to imply the existance of red and blue light shining from opposite directions. (Also see Figure 86.) Now it is a physical fact, that if two light sources (or beams of light) strike a surface and overlap each other, the overlapping area will have a brightness equal to the total sum of the two sources. The result is additive. If one beam produces 50 footlamberts and the other also 50 footlamberts, where they overlap there will be 100 footlamberts. (See top illustration, Figure 86.)

With paints and pigments, however, results will be subtractive. Overlapping areas will be darker than the paints that form them. (See bottom illustration, Figure 86.)

And other things will take place. If the lights—or the paints—are colored, again light mixtures will be additive, and paint mixtures will be subtractive. However, lights do not intermix as do pigments. Red and green *light* mixtures will form yellow, whereas in *paints*, red and green would form brown.

In Plate XIX, the colors used are a bright red and a bright blue. These colors in lights are almost direct complements. Where they overlap (additively), the result would be a pale white with a slight tinge of lavender. In paints, the mixture of red and blue (subtractive) would form dark purple or violet.

To agree with perception, then, if red and blue are applied to three-dimensional forms *as if they were lights*, the eye will gain the impression of light. It will no longer see mere pigment but will be convinced that it is witness to an effect of illumination. The human psychology of perception will be put to work.

Plate XIX was simply done. With the red and blue established, an inter-

Figure 86. The additive and subtractive mixture of colors.

mediate pale tone was mixed. This was high in value to agree with the facts of additive color phenomena. The pale tone (an off-white lavender) was then applied to areas of the forms where the red and blue were presumed to over-lap. Red was applied to the left sides and elevations, and blue to the right.

This is an excellent example of color in three dimensions, for the same scheme carried out on a flat plane would have little meaning. Plastic form has been necessary to feature it.

Obviously, color effects such as Plate XIX could be carried out in other color combinations. I have been successful with a combination of yellow-green and tan. Almost any pair could be used. From practical experience, however, opposites or near opposites are most effective. The important thing in each case is to get the additive, or transition color light enough and true to light mixtures. This is easy if the artist will, with colored filters or pieces of colored cellophane or gelatin, see what happens when two colors in illumina-tion are made to overlap each other. He then merely needs to simulate the result in paint—or in any other material (glass, ceramic, concrete, metal, plastic). He is dealing with a visual illusion, and any substance or material is suitable. (I have done well with pile carpeting in wool.)

The wonderful thing about perception is that it frees the artist from the limitations of mediums. He does not need actual illumination to simulate light, nor lustrous surfaces for a shiny effect. He exploits perception directly and may do almost anything his heart desires.

Let us consider ways in which the eye distinguishes such color modes as luster, iridescence, luminosity. The fact that silk is more lustrous than cotton has nothing to do with the volume of light each may reflect into the eye. Cotton out in the sun does not become lustrous, nor does silk in shadow assume a matte texture. (On the outer boundaries of vision, luster may often be confused with luminosity.) Katz described luster as being "brighter than bright." As to light itself, "A color must be brighter than a white surface under the same conditions if it is to be characterized as luminous." How does one go about converting these observations and findings to artistic purposes?

Plate XX offers demonstrations of two unusual effects, one of luster and the other of iridescence, applied to three-dimensional forms and photo-graphed in color. To show the great independence of perception from the materials it sees, bear in mind that the original models were made of wood, coated with paints, photographed on film which contained dye, and eventually printed with transparent inks. Yet the visual effects held true throughout.

Figure 87. An effect of luster.

In the upper illustration of Plate XX is an effect of luster—and quite convincing. The paints used on the models are not, of course, lustrous—nor were the printing inks used in the reproduction. What has contributed to the exceptionally high brightness which the eye experiences?

According to the psychologist, colors may be made to appear lustrous through the device of *black* contrast. (If the reader wants more details, he should refer to *Creative Color.*) If, for example, a series of bright colors was slightly modified with a small amount of black, the eye might assume that it was somewhat in shadow. This over-all quality of dimness would establish a "field size" against which the eye could then make comparisons. Now with pure colors applied (or added) in lesser areas, these touches would seem to be, as Katz put it, "brighter than bright." (See Figure 87 in black and white.)

In the upper illustration of Plate XX, this is how the effect was carried out. The forms, to begin with, were coated in pure yellow, yellow-green, blue-green and blue. Deeper shades of the same hues (the original color plus black) were then airbrushed as shadows. While the transitions were continuous, the same result could be achieved with flat areas. One would need merely to scale the pure colors (in 3 or 4 steps) toward black—nothing more—and apply them in flat panels which receded, curved, or took other three-dimensional form. Luster would be manifest.

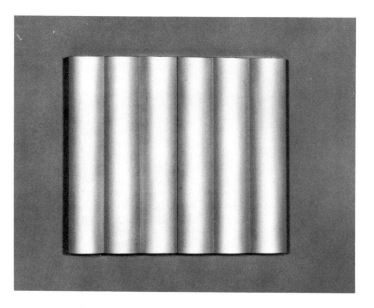

Figure 88. An effect of iridescence.

As with the demonstration of red and blue light in Plate XIX, the result is far better in relief than on a flat plane. There is also more subtlety as the viewer moves from side to side or as daylight illumination shifts.

If the upper illustration in Plate XX seems on the gaudy side, now examine the lower one. Here the effect is iridescent, and the colors used are pastel tints of yellow, orange, pink and lavender.

Most iridescence in nature, by the way—butterfly wings, seashells, opals, oil on water—does not owe its beauty to pigments but to the refraction, dispersion or scattering of light. Such "mother-of-pearl" effects also have a glimmering quality that shifts when seen at different angles—a most difficult effect to achieve with static forms. Nonetheless, the artist can simulate it. (See Figure 88 in black and white.)

Whereas luster requires black contrast, iridescence needs *gray* contrast. The iridescent touches—to establish a proper field size—must be (a) the lightest areas in view, and (b) they must be the purest areas. Where conventional scales of color usually run from pure darks to pale lights, lustrous scales run from grayish darks to pure lights.

In the lower illustration of Plate XX, the forms were painted in the pure pastels. Soft, grayish tones of the same hues were then mixed and airbrushed as shown. And once again, the eye (and perception) puts it all together to experience an uncommon beauty.

Luster and iridescence could be combined in the same plastic forms, for both phenomena are related. Near elements could take the stronger effect, and far (or lofty) elements could take the softer one. A single color or a series of colors could be handled this way. From full luster to soft iridescence, one also senses the possibility of implying aerial perspective. Groups of forms or buildings could be impressively harmonized and coordinated with each other.

In Plate XXI are two illustrations of what I take the liberty of calling Dobosh (layer cake) architecture. These are typical of the box type edifices found in American cities. Structures like these are built to enclose space, are simple in engineering principle, and are more or less economically conceived to rent at a profit. They hide nothing, disguise little, and are just as a person sees them—with little imagination involved. They may be called buildings with flesh and bones, but no soul.

Plate XXI attempts to introduce effects of luster and iridescence—one on a horizontal plane and one on a vertical in the spandrels between windows. Luster has been applied at the left in horizontal lines scaling from red to yellow. At the right the effect is one of iridescence and scales from blue to yellow. In both models the shading has been arbitrarily applied, one toward black and one toward gray to carry out principles previously described.

Perhaps these color effects appear to clash with the forms they cover. The functional architect who favors the stark and point-blank school of design may raise an eyebrow. If so, I apologize to him. I have tried to add some animation and spirit to an otherwise stolid countenance.

Effects of luster or iridescence are not difficult and could be applied to many materials such as facing tile, glazed brick, terra cotta, porcelain enamel on steel or aluminum, glass, precast stone, plastics, and so on. They would lend glory to man's recent achievements in the invention of coloring mediums.

The important thing, however, is that color could introduce perceptual factors in buildings which are visually matter-of-fact. Of course, a lot depends on whether art forms like these should have an emotional quality. I believe they should naturally, for pleasure as a necessary complement to utility has become a part of modern life. The world needs ideals and fancies and not facts alone.

In Plate XXII, the principle of chromatic light is illustrated. This effect is definitely related to the phenomenon of color constancy.

As was described in the previous chapter, the eye maintains an awareness of genuine color under widely different conditions of light intensity or *chromatic tint*. It can tell the difference between a painted red surface and a white surface illuminated by red light, and even though the illuminated red has stronger chroma than the painted red. (In this instance, of course, white would still appear to be white, regardless of the quality of light striking it.)

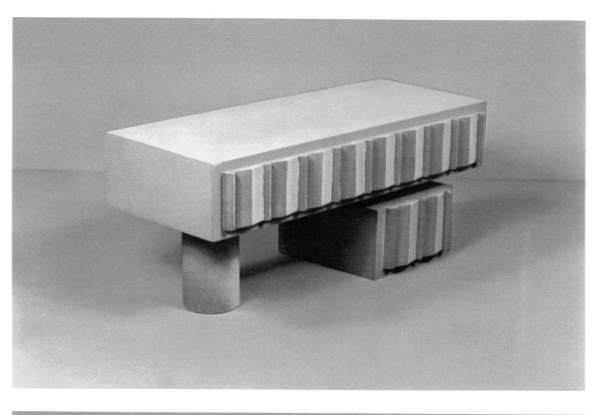

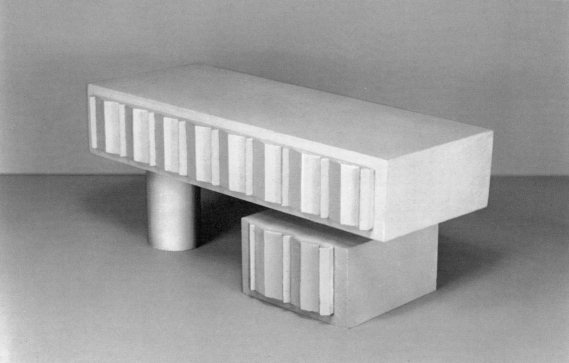

PLATE XIX. An effect of luminosity applied to simple architectural forms in three dimensions. To carry out the phenomena of light mixtures, the model was painted as if showered with red light from one direction and with blue light from the other. The result is an unusual visual experience—and it will shift as a person moves from side to side. (See page 108.)

What is remarkable from the viewpoint of perception, is that the process may be reversed. Colors applied as if under chromatic light will appear as such when seen under normal light. The effect is quite startling, for it seems to contradict external facts. The luminous beauty of many great paintings is due to such an accomplishment.

In the upper illustration of Plate XXII, one sees an architectural form under the influence of yellow illumination. In the lower illustration, green illumination is indicated.

There are a few important points to make about these chromatic light compositions. Seen in natural light, they hold great visual fascination, for the eye will be more intrigued by such illumination effects than it will be by mere schemes involving a group of colored patterns.

If genuine colors were flooded with chromatic light and seen at night, the eye would know instantly. But if the effects, as in Plate XXII, were flooded at night with ordinary artificial sources, the dynamic properties of the illusion would take over.

As a technical matter, pigments do not react on pigments in the same way that colored lights react on them. In other words, one could not arrange a group of simple colors, spray them with a transparent coating, and gain the right effect. Yellow paint over blue paint would produce green, whereas yellow *light* over blue *paint* will tend to make the paint a deep and rather muddy olive or gray. Other similar reactions would occur among other color combinations.

In Plate XXII, the palettes for yellow and green were developed by studying the actual influence of chromatic light on pigmented hues. (The materials of the artist could be of any substance, by the way.) The results were then matched in paints. Due to the workings of color constancy, human perception will piece things together and "see" tinted light where no such light exists.

There is nothing particularly difficult in this. Elaborate color schemes are often designed with ceramics, mosaics, glass, paints and enamels, and the artist may spend a good part of his time on color arrangement. Were he to step from a color scheme to a color effect, to exploit the principle of chromatic light, he could get perception busy and treat the public to visual experiences it has not had before—but which it would understand and relish on sight (perhaps like a man who witnesses Indian Summer for the first time). Pleasure in color is a gift of life and never has to be explained. Indeed, perception is a deep well from which man may draw new sensations unknown to his ancestors.

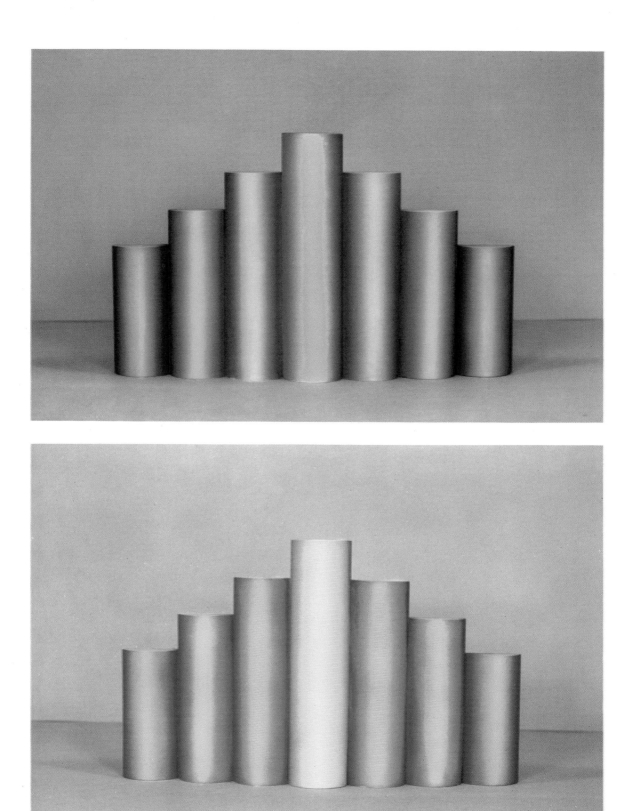

PLATE XX. Here are two convincing effects of luster (top) and iridescence (bottom) applied to three-dimensional forms. Although the results are quite realistic, the shading was arbitrarily applied in advance before the forms were photographed. Color can be made to add plasticity and new concepts of beauty which are integral with shape. (See page 110.)

PLATE XXI. Effects of luster (left) and iridescence (right) applied to conventional multi-story buildings. The dramatic application of color could do much to complement and enhance strictly functional architecture. It would add emotional appeal to forms which are more or less rational and cold in conception. (See page 113.)

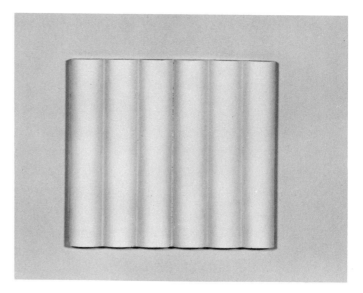

Figure 89. An effect of luminosity.

From effects of chromatic light, a further step and refinement may be made toward what I call chromatic mist. This principle combines that of luster, iridescence, chromatic light and luminosity, all in one advanced expression of beauty. (See Plate XXIII and Figure 89.)

In perception, luminous areas or objects are distinguished by the fact that they appear brighter than normal, that is, they seem so. And this brightness is achieved by subtle contrast with a grayish field or background. Where the luminous spot or area is chromatic, it further tends to cast its influence over its surrounding.

Not many artists are aware that when light shines into the eye, it causes a certain glare in vision. This glare will reduce the contrast of adjacent things. White light, for example, shining in a black field would turn the black to a medium or deep gray. Red light, placed against a green surround, would "flare" over the green and neutralize it. Thus, while light sources may actually have a high brightness ratio as against the area that lies about them, in perception the contrast appears soft. (A really bright light would more or less blind the eye to anything else.)

Written accounts of such phenomena may not make much sense. One must see for himself to understand and appreciate them. Thus Plate XXIII demonstrates this type of color effect.

There is an over-all effect of chromatic blue light, drenched in apparent mist. The model may seem to have an underwater quality. The tones used are grayish, suppressed, and provide an ideal field against which luminous touches may be made to shine forth convincingly. These luminous touches comprise a yellow, a pink, and a green which shade into purples and blues on the lowest stage. Everything is well planned and coordinated, and human perception gets busy to put into the model what actually isn't there—luminosity.

The model in Plate XXIII has been given a monumental form, not unlike a fountain. It could be less pretentious, could have other shape, be broken up with windows or otherwise adapted to most any form. The significant point is that an effect of chromatic mist has been gained which departs quite a bit from usual concepts of color arrangement.

In Plate XXIII, the eye adds many interpretations. First of all, it converts ordinary coloring material (paints in the original models, printing inks in the reproduction) to chromatic light. It tends to assume that the forms are different (possibly gray or white) from the colors that flood them. There is a notable freedom here, for perception is released from the literal to the imaginative, and the artist is able to do creative things with color.

The color organization of Plate XXIII is similar to that of Plate XXI in my book, *Creative Color*, and will not be repeated here except in a very general way. Blue is the key, although not much of it is shown. It provides the note or base from which the luminous areas unfold. This blue, in three steps, is soft in quality (and was, in fact, studied as a normal white, gray and black under the influence of blue chromatic mist).

Now, the luminous yellow, orange, pink and purple toward the left, and green, blue and purple toward the right were applied as shown in confined touches. What gives the whole composition its unity and conviction lies in the fact that the colors which appear luminous were also studied under the influence of blue chromatic mist. This influence was then matched in paints (to equal what transpired), and the eye has put the whole together for a singular and impressive act of perception.

The color effect of Plate XXIII could take any arrangement of hues and have any key other than blue. This is true, indeed, of all the principles so far described: the simulation of colored light to model form; luster; iridescence; chromatic light; chromatic mist; luminosity. Once the architect or designer thinks inwardly of perception rather than outwardly of color as a mere surface, he may set himself free to work with color almost as a musician works with chords and rhythms to tap emotional responses which lie deep in the human psyche.

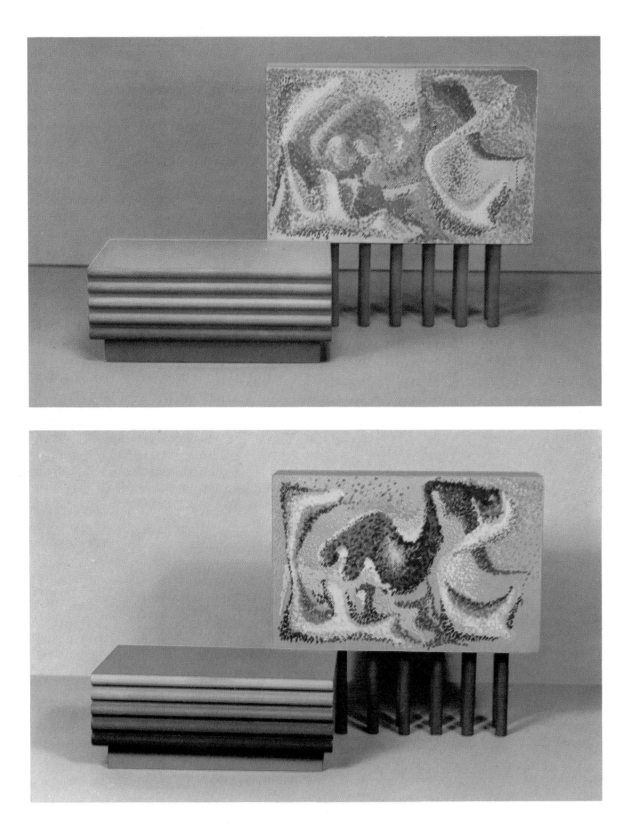

PLATE XXII. Effects of chromatic light in yellow (above) and green (below) as applied to architectural forms. What is unusual is that the eye senses a tinted quality of light that is foreign to the general illumination in the field of view. Perception is put to work in the interest of creative invention. (See page 113.)

PLATE XXIII. *This singular effect is meant to convey an impression of forms which are self-luminous, but which, in reality, are illuminated from outside. There would be a difference in human perception. Beauty of color which is inherent with form and material is to be commended, for it requires skill and knowledge on the part of the artist that goes beyond the superficial. (See page 118.)*

Figure 90. An effect of transparency gained with ceramic tile.

Now go to Plate XXIV and Figure 90. Even such a simple visual experience as transparency has perceptional elements which may be implied in fully opaque materials. Both the upper illustration of Plate XXIV and Figure 90 were done with ordinary ceramic mosaic.

Probably related to the phenomenon of color constancy, transparency is an interpretation of eye and mind and does not depend upon the actual existence of transparent materials in its field of view. For that matter, if the seemingly transparent areas of Plate XXIV and Figure 90 were literally transparent, the eye could spot the situation at once. What is unusual about the demonstration is that the eye, aware that it is looking at *opaque* surfaces, still sees them as *transparent* anyhow! It finds the illusion quite engaging.

This effect, simple though it is, has seldom been applied—except by chance. Floor patterns of tile, rubber, vinyl, linoleum could feature it. Ceramic or enamel murals could likewise be given novelty and strong visual and emotional interest.

For that matter, large buildings and structures could display the idea. This is indicated in the lower illustration of Plate XXIV. While color in itself holds a sure compulsion, an effect of transparent color would be all the more intriguing, for it would demand participation in the result and enable the designer to go far beyond the mere choice of colors or the mere placement of colors in some conventional or unconventional arrangement.

Perceptionism in architecture, decoration and the plastic arts is at a beginning. This book has endeavored to set forth the findings of the Gestalt psychologist and researcher in vision and—within the limitations of process color reproduction—to make esthetic and practical demonstrations. It is hoped that what may seem theoretical and experimental in these pages, will one day become practical realities in the architectural and plastic arts of the future.

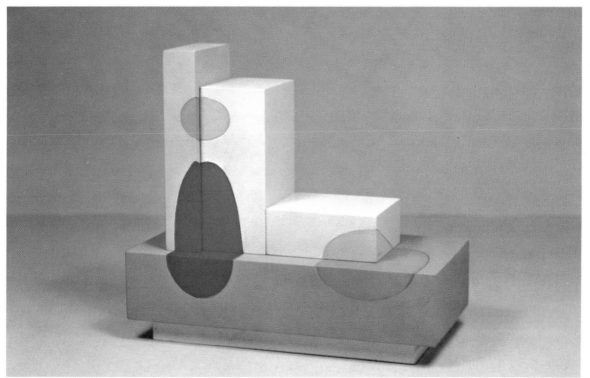

PLATE XXIV. Two effects of transparency applied with wholly opaque materials. In the mural (above) and the architectural form (below), transparency as a visual phenomenon is successfully achieved. The principle involved is a simple one and could do wonders to dramatize the beauty of two-dimensional or three-dimensional areas.

Bibliography

The sources listed below cover major references only. All are good books or articles to consult on color and form. The author has purposely avoided the inclusion of incidental and miscellaneous items from which only a sentence or two have been quoted. Complete bibliographies on the subject of color will be found in other works by the author.

Allport, Floyd H., *Theories of Perception and the Concept of Structure*, John Wiley & Sons, New York, 1955.

Arnheim, Rudolf, *Art and Visual Perception*, University of California Press, Berkeley, 1957.

Birren, Faber, *Color Psychology and Color Therapy*, McGraw-Hill Book Co., New York, 1950.

Birren, Faber, "The Emotional Significance of Color Preference," *American Journal of Occupational Therapy*, March-April, 1952.

Birren, Faber, *New Horizons in Color*, Reinhold Publishing Corp., New York, 1955.

Birren, Faber, "The Effects of Color on the Human Organism," *American Journal of Occupational Therapy*, May-June, 1959.

Birren, Faber, *Creative Color*, Reinhold Publishing Corp., New York, 1961.

Bragdon, Claude, *Projective Ornament*, Manas Press, Rochester, 1915.

Bragdon, Claude, *The New Image*, Alfred A. Knopf, New York, 1928.

Gibson, James J., *The Perception of the Visual World*, Houghton Mifflin Co., Cambridge, 1950.

Goldstein, Kurt, *The Organism*, American Book Co., New York, 1939.

Gombrich, E. H., *Art and Illusion*, Pantheon Books, New York, 1960.

Hambidge, Jay, *Practical Applications of Dynamic Symmetry*, Yale University Press, New Haven, 1932.

Hambidge, Jay, *The Elements of Dynamic Symmetry*, Yale University Press, New Haven, 1948.

Hayek, F. A., *The Sensory Order*, University of Chicago Press, Chicago, 1952.

Katz, David, *The World of Colour*, Kegan Paul, Trench, Trubner & Co., London, 1935.

Katz, David, *Gestalt Psychology*, Ronald Press, New York, 1950.

Katz, David, *Animals and Men*, Penguin Books, London, 1953.

Kepes, Gyorgy, *Language of Vision*, Paul Theobald & Co., Chicago, 1959.

Koffka, Kurt, *Principles of Gestalt Psychology*, Harcourt, Brace & Co., New York, 1935.

Köhler, Wolfgang, *Gestalt Psychology*, Liveright Publishing Corp., New York, 1947.

Moholy-Nagy, L., *Vision in Motion*, Paul Theobald & Co., Chicago, 1947.

Ostwald, Wilhelm, *Die Harmonie der Formen*, Verlag Unesma, Leipzig, 1922.

Vernon, M. D., *A Further Study of Visual Perception*, Cambridge University Press, London, 1954.

Werner, Heinz, *Comparative Psychology of Mental Development*, Follett Publishing Corp., Chicago, 1948.

Index